SPEAKING ACTIVITIES THAT DON'T SUCK

By English Teacher X

Copyright © 2011 by English Teacher X

For further information please contact the author at englishteacherx@yahoo.com

Visit the author at www.englishteacherx.com:

Twitter: www.twitter.com/@englishteacherx

Facebook: www.facebook.com/englishteacherx

Contents

Consider your personal answers to the following questions. Do you agree or disagree with these statements?

1) My students, like dead hookers, should be seen and not heard.

2) I believe that my students need to spend the whole class reading, listening, and writing, because I am usually too hungover to want to speak.

3) My students are too fucking stupid to talk.

4) The class is most interesting when I'm telling them funny stories about all the cool stuff that happened to me back when I was a backpacker.

5) My students don't want to speak. They thrive on silence.

6) I consistently come up with brilliant speaking activities and fascinating topics, and yet still my students sit there like little mushrooms.

7) Sometimes I wish I was back at the Barnes & Noble, where I didn't have people staring at me like mental patients all the time.

8) Like testicle cancer, there is simply no way to make English class enjoyable.

9) I need to correct every single fucking mistake that the little bastards make. It's my only reason to exist.

10) If a student hasn't started crying by the end of the class, I feel empty inside.

Okay…have you considered your answers? Is your moment of reflection complete?

Then let's begin.

INTRODUCTION: ANSWER ME WHEN I TELL YOU TO SHUT UP!

MORE ASS SHOWING

I often envy baboons.

They communicate by screeching, hitting each other, and showing each other their asses.

Humans don't have it so easy.

We have an extremely complicated system of social interaction and communication based on spoken word, social mores and customs, body language, and intonation.

Little wonder humans have so much trouble getting along. The world needs more ass-showing and screeching!

Alas, you, the Teacher of English as a Foreign Language, henceforth referred to as the teacher, You, or the dumbfuck, have the unenviable job of teaching your students to communicate.

The one thing that history has shown us that all humans are pretty much uniformly terrible at.

OH SHIT

Calm down.

A few things to remember first.

Let's narrow your job down a little.

First of all, your job isn't to teach the students to communicate. Not really.

It's just to teach them to SPEAK.

There will be some presentation and exchange of ideas here, of course, but we're mostly concerned with the act of speaking itself, not some kind of meaningful dialogue.

ANY MORON CAN SPEAK

Most human beings can speak, except of course for Harpo Marx, Snake Eyes on GI Joe, and Helen Keller and her noble brothers and sisters.

Unfortunately, pretty much none of them have anything interesting, relevant, or meaningful to say.

Now I come from a different generation – I started teaching in 1995 – when the ability to speak English was widely considered to be the only qualification necessary to be able to teach English.

Most native speakers got through their lessons in one of two ways:

1) They read to the students from the book.

2) They told the students stories about their lives and daily activities.

Or some combination of the two. In Asia, especially, this was generally accepted just fine.

But alas, about 2000 or so, the world started to seriously Globalize. Fast internet came along. People from developing countries started traveling more.

They began to realize they hadn't learned a fucking thing from listening to that florid-faced Australian guy stand in front of the class reading and telling funny stories.

And anyway – you aren't being paid enough to be a standup comedian. If you like telling funny stories, you're wasting it on foreign students, who can't understand you anyway.

If you like reading aloud, consider becoming a television news presenter. Or a politician.

YOU'RE TEACHING GYM, NOT HISTORY

So the thing to remember here:

SPEAKING IS A PHYSICAL SKILL, like swimming or playing football.

Could you learn to swim by watching YouTube videos of people swimming?

No, you gotta go out there and get your ass wet as much as possible.

So remember, you're teaching a skill here, and you have to make the students practice that skill.

BUT LET'S DO A LITTLE MATH HERE

Okay, they probably told you as much in your CELTA class, if you took one.

You're in a class with 12 students. You speak individually to each of those 12 students, over the course of one hour.

Quick, how much time did each student speak?

That's right. 2.5 minutes, assuming that you spoke half the time and the students each spoke half the time.

Could you learn to swim with 2.5 minutes in the water, three times a week?

Of course not.

"Pair work!" is often the magic word spoken by training courses, to mitigate this time deficiency.

See, you put your students in pairs to do the activities, and that will increase the amount of time they can speak.

And you? What should you be doing?

Your job is to walk around and listen for typical mistakes, answer students' questions, make suggestions, give feedback, and all that hippie crap.

(In reality you can just walk around and nod thoughtfully and that'll be about all you need to do.)

So your job is to shut up and let the students talk.

BLOOD FROM A STONE

Sure! Students will be more comfortable speaking to each other, probably. They'll be speaking to someone with a more similar background and interests. It'll be more realistic communication, right?

But what they don't spend enough time teaching you in CELTA courses is what the students are going to talk ABOUT.

Here's a little feedback loop you'll often hear:

"Okay, class, today we're going to talk about oil pollution."

Utter silence.

Teacher tries gamely to ask a few questions and gets minimal responses while the kids in the back send text messages and talk in their native language.

"Okay, get in pairs and ask some questions about oil pollution."

Silence. Sound of ANGRY BIRDS being played on iPhones.

Finally one smartass pipes up: "Teacher, this topic is boring."

"Okay, what do you want to talk about?"

"I don't know. You're the teacher."

Sometimes the teacher makes a misguided attempt to salvage the class by adopting a topic HE considers interesting.

"Okay, let's get rid of this boring book. Let's talk about UFOs!"

One student says, "I very liked X-FILES."

"Anybody here ever seen a UFO?" asks the teacher.

Everyone shakes their heads.

"Anybody know any interesting stories about UFOs?"

Everyone continues to shake their heads; at least, everyone who can be bothered to look up from playing ANGRY BIRDS.

"Er, uh, get into pairs…and…uh…?" says the teacher.

Silence.

"Okay let's just do a writing activity…" says the teacher, finally.

The students groan and say no, no, let's do a speaking activity!

"What do you want to talk about?" asks the teacher, wanting to cry.

"I don't know. You're the teacher."

After class the teacher bitches and moans in the staffroom about how retarded his students are.

So it's not usually the topic; it's how you PREPARE the students for the topic, and how carefully you guide them, cow-like, to the language you want them to produce.

WHY WE'RE HERE

I am going to teach you how to forcefully extract coherent responses out of your students to all manner of simple (and more advanced) conversational questions, at all levels, with techniques and activities that you can do with minimal or no preparation.

And we're even going to do it without waterboards.

PART ONE:

THE ANATOMY OF AN ENGLISH LESSON

In which we look at the bits and pieces which assemble the grotesque corpse of a TEFL lesson, and examine some ways to force students to speak during the usual robotic course of business

MORE QUESTIONS FOR PERSONAL DEVELOPMENT AND STUFF

Consider the answers to these questions. Go ahead, make some notes even. I'll wait.

1) Think of the five main reasons that you suck as an English teacher.

2) Why do you speak so much in class, you dumbass?

3) Why are your lessons so boring and stupid? Try to think of at least five reasons.

4) What are your usual feeble methods for getting the students to speak in class, when you can even be bothered to do so?

5) Consider your usual methods of getting the students to speak – why are those methods so pitiful and unsuccessful, leading to nothing but complaints and silence?

6) Consider all the reasons that you hate your students and enumerate them here.

7) Do you REALLY think that your students are stupid, and have absolutely nothing to say, or is that a case of an inferior craftsman blaming his tools?

WHY YOU SUCK AS A TEFL TEACHER

I'm sure students complain about you all the time.

If they don't complain to your face, or you don't hear about it from your administration, you probably work in a place where there aren't many other English teachers available to replace you. Lucky you.

Now, they probably complain about one of two things:

1) You're boring.

2) They can't understand you.

In both cases, you're just talking too fucking much.

So, put those little bastards to work!

MAKE THOSE FUCKERS TALK!

In the first part, I'm going to look at the general structure of a typical class, and illustrate some ways to make students talk so much that they won't ever dare complain they're bored.

DECONSTRUCTING A TEFL LESSON

Every lesson is NOT different. While all the CONTENT of the activities is different, the TYPES of activities are very similar.

Most lessons can be broken down into the following parts. Apply these formulas to the TYPES of activities, and you barely need a lesson plan.

Now generally, I'm talking about a class based on a course book. Later, I'll give you some advice for creating a whole speaking lesson with no book and no materials.

Every course-book based lesson will probably have the following parts:

- **A warmer**, which is a short activity or activities, to kick off the class.

- **The body of the lesson**, which probably consists of activities from your text book, usually with a mixture of skills including **reading, listening, grammar, and speaking.** (Writing activities are often given for homework.)

- **A closer**, which is some activity or set way to end the class.

We'll look at each of them, and how to force students to speak during each of them.

THE FIRST PART: THE WARMER

A warmer will be defined as a quick, usually easy, usually speaking-based activity to review something students have already done, or occasionally, to introduce a new topic.

Class begins with a warmer for two reasons:

1) To begin the class with a light-hearted, enjoyable speaking activity to gently lead the students into speaking English and review some things you've already done in the past.

(Enjoyable is pretty relative, of course – these activities will be more enjoyable than a brain tumor, but considerably less enjoyable than a deep-tissue massage from a bisexual Lebanese 20-year-old.)

2) To let the late students arrive. Chronic lateness is a problem at just about any private language school, and because they're paying students,

it's unlikely there will be any way to punish them. So you would just have to go back and repeat whatever information you gave at the beginning of class, and that would be annoying.

How long should you spend on warmers? It depends on the length of your course, how much material from the book you are obliged to cover, etc. Could be anywhere from five minutes to 30 minutes.

(The speaking activities in Part Two of the book can make excellent warmers, as reviews of topics that students have already studied. That's what we professional authors call "foreshadowing.")

Here are some typical activities that can be done as warmers with minimal preparation on your part.

1) ASK YOUR PARTNER FIVE (10, 20) QUESTIONS

Get students to talk about a topic, or in a particular grammatical form you've done.

Put the students in pairs and say,

You:

"Ask your partner five questions about last weekend" or "next weekend" or "Ask your partner five questions about your family" (or whatever topic you want to review.)

Students hopefully go to work; this will be a considerable task for pre-intermediate students, a light and breezy pleasure for intermediate or advanced students.

For very basic students, you might offer some help:

Board:

What / mother / name? Father? Brother? Sister?

What / mother's / age? Job? Address? Hair color? (Etc.)

Or whatever. All of this will be discussed in graphic and thrilling detail in Part Two.

You walk around and listen and nod and all that.

After a few minutes, you ask a few questions to random students, or have them ask you random questions.

I might advise you to take note of a particular problem that might crop up: a student will say, "Teacher, we asked about family last week."

To which you should respond, "AND YOU'LL KEEP ASKING ABOUT FAMILY UNTIL IT'S ABSOLUTELY PERFECT!" Tell them talking about the same shit again and again is a VERY IMPORTANT PART of English language communication.

2) VOCABULARY PRACTICE

Reviewing vocabulary through speaking can be a good warmer.

For elementary students, they probably have "picture dictionaries" in their book to present basic vocabulary. You need to review that shit a lot.

You:

"Okay, open your books to page _____" – to the pictures of classroom objects (or whatever.)

"Now ask your partner, 'What's this?' and answer, 'It's a…'"

Demonstrate with some cute chick in the front row.

Students get into pairs.

Student A: "What's this?"

Student B: "It's a pen."

Student A: "Fascinating. What's this?"

Or look at pictures of people in a magazine. You hand out some pictures or magazines to the students.

You: "Get into pairs."

Board the question, perhaps:

Board:

What's his / her job?

Student A: "What's his job?"

Student B: "He's a doctor. What are you, blind?"

Etc., etc. More about the glory of pictures later.

If you don't have the pictures, you could write the words you want to review on the board, and use a different question. Very basic students could translate:

You:

"Okay – now ask your partner the question – what does ____ mean in (your native language)?"

Board:

Pen

Pencil

Paper

(Etc.)

Student A: "What does apple mean in Blkrgeneze?"

Student B: "It's a xccbrusbboweisn."

You can do spelling activities here:

Student A: "How do you spell pens?"

Student B: "P – E – N – I – S."

Student A: "No I said…"

As always – demonstrate with a hot chick first, and then have them do it in pairs, and then have them ask you a question.

This can go as fast or slow as need be. The difference between a beginner and an advanced student is more speed and various asides or extra material, not the basic topic.

3) INFORMATION GAP / PHOTOCOPIED SHIT

Most schools have an abundance of books full of photocopied activities, especially nonsensical "information gap" activities.

Personally I don't like these because they involve photocopying and that's too much like actually preparing.

But you might have some left over from another class, or maybe you didn't have time to get around to something the day before, or whatever, so occasionally they have their uses.

Just try to make sure it is something they've already studied, eh?

Reduce, reuse, repeat, reiterate, recycle, and regurgitate.

THE SECOND PART: THE BODY

The body of a lesson, usually taken from your course book, will consist of the following:

Reading

Listening

Speaking

Grammar Activities

Although – remember – these things will happen in various orders. There's no particular rule that grammar has to come before speaking, or whatever. Or hell, even omit one. I don't care.

Extended writing activities are usually given for homework, but you might want to whip one out occasionally if you've got a bad hangover.

One thing to remember is that it's very easy to turn ANYTHING into a pairwork speaking activity, mostly through a useful (for once) CELTA-class concept that actually works pretty well and in addition takes up plenty of class time.

PAIR CHECK FIRST, THEN GROUP CHECK! ALWAYS!!

Think of this as the "TEFL Class Activity Rule of Three":

1) Students do some activity individually (or perhaps just think about what they're going to do).

2) Students do or check the activity in pairs.

3) Students check the answer across the class with the teacher smiling benevolently and bringing the light of knowledge into the world.

This has a few advantages, which you might want to share with the students:

1) It makes sure stupid kids can catch up.

2) It gives the smart students plenty of time to practice.

3) Students can interact, rather than just watching your dumb hungover ass.

READING

Typically, in a course book, students read a text on some bland multi-culturally acceptable subject and then complete comprehension / vocabulary questions of one kind or another.

After the students are finished, tell them to check their answers with the person sitting next to them.

You:

"Okay...when you are finished with the text, answer the questions."

(Ten minutes later.)

"Now, speak to your partner. Check the answers to your questions, and ask your partner why they chose that answer."

Simplify it for BEGINNER STUDENTS:

You:

"Okay, check your answers."

Board:

What's the correct answer to # _____? Why? Which line number?

(This assumes the text you're using has line numbers – usually the correct answer is the question of finding which line the answer is in.)

Again, the pair work promotes hippie stuff like group dynamics and morale, and allows the smart students to explain stuff to the stupid ones.

So you don't have to.

(What's more – this will actually force students to do the reading and not just circle a random answer.)

Now, for elementary students, you can let them pair check in their native language first.

Or you can have them read the questions and answers to each other, before you do it as a class. (That is, if there is a simple text with multiple choice questions and answers, have students read the question to their partner, the partner reads the full answer, and then switch for the next one.

You:

"Okay, now – get into pairs – Student A, read the question to number one. Student B, read the correct answer. Then switch. If you don't agree, you can say – "

Board:

I'm sorry, I don't agree. I think _____ is correct.

Whoop bang! Killing time and producing English.

With more advanced classes, you can think of extra activities.

You can have them explain vocabulary words from the reading to each other in English.

You:

"Choose 10 words that you think are interesting or important from this text. Point at the word, and ask your partner."

Board:

What does this word mean?

How do you pronounce it?

Or just have the students close their books and try to remember what they read and tell their partner the main points of it.

You:

"Look at the first three paragraphs. Okay, now close your book. Explain to your partner the main idea of what you read."

"Now, the second partner reads the next three paragraphs. Same thing – explain what you read."

Having one student read aloud while the others listen, like you did in kindergarten, is pretty boring and stupid, and not something you should do too often – only occasionally, for pronunciation.

You can do other stuff on that theme, though.

You:

"Okay, read the first paragraph to your partner. Partner, listen. If you hear any pronunciation problems, wait until your partner is finished reading and then correct him."

Board:

Excuse me…I think that word is pronounced…

You know, pit them against each other so they won't gang up on you.

Divide and conquer, and all that.

I've heard this kind of thing referred to as "exploiting the material" and I like that, because it brings to mind torture and abuse.

And we're all about torture and abuse here.

LISTENING

Basically the same procedure as the reading. Remember the good old RULE OF THREE.

Students will listen to something, and then answer some questions individually. (Sometimes they will listen twice before they answer the questions – use your own stellar judgment.)

But basically the form of it will be similar to reading – they'll listen to some kind of dry lecture or tepid conversation, and then have to answer multiple choice questions or gap fills, or whatever.

You:

"Okay. Now check your answers, in English, with your partner."

Board:

What's the correct answer to number…? Why?

Again, simplify it for elementary and beginner:

You:

"Okay, read question number one to your partner. Student B will read the answer. Complete sentences!"

Again, with advanced students, you can think of a million other activities.

Have them listen once with their books closed.

You:

"Okay, now, talk with your partner. Tell your partner what you remember about what you heard."

Then they can listen again with books open, looking at the questions.

You:

"Now check your answers in English."

"What's the correct answer? Why? "

You're starting to get the drill, right?

A common trick it to let them read a transcript of what they heard, to check the answers, and then you can go back and do some of the reading activities already mentioned.

Reduce, recycle, reuse, repeat, reiterate, redo, regurgitate.

GRAMMAR

Part Two will present plenty of activities to practice different grammar forms. It's kind of difficult to separate grammar and speaking, no matter what that nutty old woman in your CELTA class told you.

Again though: RULE OF THREE.

Some general advice:

DON'T EXPLAIN GRAMMAR RULES, or at least DON'T READ FROM THE BOOK.

If the rules are presented clearly in the book, ask the students to read the rules, and explain them to you.

Again, do it just like the reading.

You:

"Read the grammar rules."

. . .

"Okay, now, get into pairs, close your book, and tell your partner what you remember."

Now, in low-level classes, you could do something like this:

You:

"Look at the grammar rules. Explain these rules to your partner in your native language."

Then they do the grammar activities, gap fills, or writing sentences, or whatever.

The same drill! Rule of three!

You:

"Check the answers in pairs with your partner. Look back at the grammar rules."

Board:

What's the correct answer?

Or

Is this correct? Why?

This is the part where the smart kids really come in handy explaining stuff to the stupid kids. A little native language can go a long way here.

When checking as a group, make sure you have the students read the complete sentences, at least. That's kind of like speaking.

Avoid this type of thing:

You: "Number one?"

Students: "Did."

You: "Number two?"

Students: "Was."

Better:

You: "Miss Su, read the complete sentence in grammar question number two. WITH FEELING!"

Also, look at the grammar activities the students are doing. Often there are various ways to exploit them through speaking.

Are they questions, for example?

Often they are in the form of gap fills – for example, students have to complete:

"What time _____ you get up yesterday?"

"Where _____ you yesterday at 5:30 pm?"

After you have established the correct answer, as explained above, you could have the students ask each other the questions, and ANSWER them.

You:

"Okay, complete the questions in Exercise Three. Now ask your partner the questions. Partner, answer in a full sentence."

Whoa, English in action! Or inaction.

And of course – in Part Two – I have a huge number of speaking activities related to all sorts of grammatical forms.

As far as explaining grammar, that's usually by WRITING EXAMPLES ON THE BOARD AND ASKING THE STUDENTS WHY. Obviously this will take a little practice and is extremely fucking difficult.

SPEAKING ACTIVITIES

The actual speaking activities in books are usually remarkably lame.

Often they'll just give you some vague instructions like, "Have a class discussion about the greenhouse effect" or "Have a class discussion about how to reduce plastic pollution."

This, as I've established, is a recipe for a lot of silence.

The book MIGHT have a list of questions related to the topic that students are supposed to discuss. The only problem with the books is that there usually aren't enough questions, and the questions aren't always suited to YOUR students.

That's where you come in.

The other typical speaking activity from the book is the INFORMATION GAP – students have pictures or maps or information, similar but not exactly the same, and must ask their partner questions to determine information.

A typical "information gap" activity would have two students with the same map, but different buildings marked.

This is supposed to encourage realistic communication as the two students try to work out the location of different buildings.

(That some CELTA instructors consider this "realistic communication" just shows you how fucking out of it THEY are. The only realistic meaningful communication in this case would be showing the other student the map.)

I detest these, as a general rule, but they are part of the brick and mortar of a text book, so you will, most likely, have to do a bit of photocopying and put them to use.

My advice is to demonstrate the activity clearly, in front of the class, with a willing student, because students, especially elementary students, are often completely befuddled by these. (And rightly so.)

CLOSER

This is a little YOU time. Teacher time. This is the last five minutes or so of class.

If you work at a place that gives homework, clearly explain, and write on the board, the students' homework for the next class. You might need to check and make sure students did their homework from the last class. (Probably they didn't.) You can ask if there are any final questions.

Usually there won't be, so you might, for example, ask a few random questions or make a few random observations or tell a funny story or whatever. (Depending on how strictly your administration expects you to stay in class until exactly the correct time of dismissal.)

Students do need to hear you speak occasionally, after all, if only so they remember you are not simply an android who walks around nodding and smiling benignly.

And occasionally stinking of alcohol.

Of course there are a lot of other ways to kill five or 10 minutes if you need to – for example, use the same kind of activities as the warmer --

something from Part Two. Or, you know, play hangman, or I Spy, or whatever.

SOME COMMON RESPONSES TO FREQUENTLY ASKED QUESTIONS

Here are some common student (and occasionally teacher) questions that arise about doing pair work.

Student: "But if I speak to another student, they won't correct my mistakes."

You: "Yeah, and it's a good thing. Because otherwise we'd never fucking get a sentence finished, you moron!"

Remind the students that George W. Bush Jr. probably never produced a grammatically correct sentence in his life, and it didn't hurt his career any.

As for accent – Schwarzenegger and Stallone did okay for themselves.

Student: "But I want to speak with you, Mr. Native Speaker!"

You: "My rate for individual lessons is much higher than you pay for the group, but I'd be happy to accept it to speak only with you."

Also, remind them that given the fact that the economies of America and Great Britain are collapsing, if they're speaking English for business purposes in the future, they're likely to be speaking English with the Chinese or the Brazilians.

PART TWO: SHORT AND EASY SPEAKING ACTIVITIES

In which we discuss some brutally efficient ways to force English from recalcitrant learners on a wide variety of common topics and to enhance their knowledge of certain arcane and inscrutable grammatical forms

STILL MORE PERSONAL GROWTH AND PROFESSIONAL SELF-IMPROVEMENT QUESTIONS

Here are some questions for you to consider, before we begin the second part.

1) Suppose you have some time to kill and you want to review the topic of "family." What would you do? Try to think of at least three activities.

2) Why were your answers to Question One so lame? Do you really consider yourself a teacher?

3) Okay, how about the past tense? Think of three short activities to review the past tense. And don't say, "Run to the office and photocopy some activity about the past tense." Something with no fucking photocopying!

4) Christ, those are terrible, why did you leave your fucking job at the Barnes & Noble, anyway?

SHORT SPEAKING ACTIVITIES: YOUR MOST EFFECTIVE WEAPON AGANST RECALCITRANCE

These activities are designed to be short – generally no more than five to 10 minutes – and to review, reinforce, and practice grammar and vocabulary points that students have already studied.

Intermediate students might find them easy and zip through them; but, having more ability, they might expand on the basic idea and take longer.

They could be used to introduce a certain grammar form or topic, with a bit of backup.

Even "elementary" activities could be used at the "advanced" level in sort of a "lightning round" with more activities crammed into a shorter period of time.

I mean, really – there is NO SUCH THING AS TOO MUCH PRACTICE OF THE BASICS. If the students mouth off about "We've studied this already," tell them that a football player does not kick the ball 10 times and proclaim himself an expert – he kicks it tens of thousands of times.

If they still object, tell them that questions such as, "How are you?" and "What did you do last weekend?" are a DAILY or WEEKLY part of conversation for native speakers, so they can practice them daily or weekly and not feel they're doing anything stupid.

Most of these activities should be carried out in the same way:

1) Review vocabulary: Go over whatever words are necessary, in the ways described below.

2) Demonstrate a few questions with a student, or students.

3) Put the students in pairs and let them do questions in pairs for a few minutes, while you walk around the room nodding sagely and answering any questions the students may ask about the fine grammar and vocabulary points of whatever they're trying to do.

Smile and be wise, professorial and confident, and try not to think about your hangover.

4) Finally, do a few questions teacher to students, students to teacher, or student to student across the classroom.

HOW TO REVIEW VOCABULARY

Many of these activities begin by reviewing a vocabulary set – food, drinks, jobs, etc. If you are using a text book, there are probably units that feature these sets. The text book may also have something like a "picture dictionary" where students have matched the words to the pictures.

If you aren't using a book, or your book doesn't have any focus on vocabulary, or you want to review words that students studied earlier but aren't in this book, you can do any of the following:

Just write on the board (for example, FOOD) and ask the students:

You: "Okay, tell me some foods…"

Students: "Apples! Quiche Lorraine! Spam! Monkey brains!"

Board: (as the students shout them out)

Apples

Quiche Lorraine

Spam

Etc.

The words you have written can be references for the activities in question.

Or you can use a ball. This will often delude the students into thinking they are doing something fun.

You:

"Okay, tell me a food in English." (Throw the ball to a student.) "Okay, tell me another food, in English." (Throw the ball to another student.)

They'll probably get the idea pretty quickly.

Or you can have them write.

You:

"Okay, get into pairs. Write down a list of 20 different (foods)."

A more detailed vocabulary review for an upper-intermediate or advanced lesson:

You:

"Get into pairs. Write down a list of 10 different fruits. (. . .) Okay, now write down a list of 10 different vegetables. (. . .) Okay, now write down a list of 10 things you can buy in a fast food restaurant."

You could do it using the ABC game.

You:

"Write down a food that begins with A."

"Now, write a food that begins with B…now C…"

Again, unless you're teaching special ed, they'll get the idea.

A WORD ABOUT CONVERSATION IN GENERAL

So, it has been mentioned in response to some of these activities, that even teachers have trouble thinking of, for example, five questions that begin with the question word "What…?"

I hope after you've read this book, you'll see that conversation is kind of about making lists. I mean, really – think about it.

A: Hey Bob, what did you do last weekend?

B: I went to the movies.

A: Oh, really, what did you see?

B: TRANSFORMERS 5.

A: How was it?

B: Man, it sucked balls.

A: Did you go with your wife or your mistress?

See, A here – his questions are pretty standard stuff. The conversation will only veer off the list, for him, if he makes an observation about something that B said. A has a list of questions in his head about movies that he can exhaustively grill B with.

You have to have some questions ready on whatever topic, and this book will provide some of those lists. He probably has a list of observations he will share, also, but that list isn't quite as firmly in his head as the list of questions about movies.

So, meaningful conversation? Or rote parroting of learned prompts and responses?

Ask the baboons, 'cause I can't tell you.

If you can't think of questions, looking at a list of common verbs will often jar your memory when you put it next to the question words.

Hopefully, reading this book will get you thinking in terms of lists.

Five questions with what:

- What is your name?

- What is your father's name?

- What are your favorite foods?

- What do you think of Chinese food?

- What is the capital of Mongolia?

Now I hope you're not so stupid that I have to point out to you that we could change one word in those questions and ask dozens of others:

- What is your address / phone number / email address?

- What is your brother's / sister's / manager's name?

- What are your favorite foods / movies / TV shows?

- What do you think of Chinese food / Toyota Corollas / the global economic crisis?

- What is the capital of Mongolia / Spain / Malaysia?

The appendix has some exercises to help you get your brain going on the subject of making questions.

HOW TO USE THESE ACTIVITIES:

Use them as warmers, or to expand on some grammar point the students are studying, or as extra activities when you've finished stuff in the book.

Or, you can piece together damn near a whole class out of them. If, for some reason, you have to teach a class without a course book, you can combine a bunch of the damn things, preferably those with some thematic relationships. And of course personalized and expanded on for your students as you see fit.

MORE THAN 50 ACTIVITIES FOR FORCING ENGLISH OUT OF YOUR STUDENTS WITH LITTLE OR NO PREPARATION

It's possible to do pretty much all of these activities with nothing more than a board and a marker, but some other optional items include:

1) A ball – a small light ball of the type given to babies or dogs. (The mentality of your students will hopefully be somewhere between these two.)

2) Pictures – there are several references to pictures. Generally speaking, you'll be using a text book that's chock full of pictures of people, of all kinds of people doing all kinds of activities; you can flip around in the book and use these to describe people, jobs, clothes, places, etc.

Lower-level books often have something like a "picture dictionary" – for example, a page with pictures of different kinds of fruit, which students have had to match to the names of fruit. Ways to EXPLOIT these are discussed in depth.

3) Interactive electronic whiteboard and PowerPoint – yeah, well, if you're lucky enough to be at a place that has that kind of shit, you probably don't need a book like this.

4) Realia: This is a teacher-trainer favorite word that means to bring in real stuff to use as "props" in your role-playing activities.

So like, for example, when doing a role play as a customs official, bring in a badge and a gun, and when you're doing a role play as a shopkeeper, bring in a full inventory of packaged goods to sell, and a real cash register.

Yeah, well, if you feel your salary justifies that kind of effort, you rock on, rock star.

5) Several of these activities mention dice, but ways to do them without dice are also mentioned. I myself generally don't bother to bring dice to class anymore.

Now, the presentation of the activities should be clear.

You:

Will be followed by what you're going to say in class.

Board:

Will be followed by what you're going to write on the board.

1) DICE QUESTIONS

LEVEL: All

This is a general review of question forms. It's basically good for any level, because the students can decide how easy or complex the question is.

Board:

1) What

2) Where

3) When

4) Why

5) Who

6) How

Give students dice.

You: "Okay, get in pairs. Roll the dice and make some questions for your partner with the correct question word."

Do it yourself a couple of times to demonstrate:

E.g. after rolling 6, ask a student, "How are you today?"

and after rolling 5 ask:

You: "Who is your favorite actor?"

Hot Chick: "Brad Pitt, of course, although he's older than my dad now."

Let them practice for 5-10 minutes, and then you can do some as a class.

(The students can make the questions as easy or as difficult as they wish.)

ELEMENTARY: "What are your favorite colors?"

INTERMEDIATE: "What do you do in the evenings?"

ADVANCED: "What are your feelings about the current situation in Krkmnenstan?"

This is sometimes surprisingly difficult, so you might need to offer a few skeletons of questions to help them along.

Board:

Who is your favorite…?

What time do you…?

How much is a…?

Why do you…?

When do you usually…?

Where is…?

Helpful Hint: You can do this easily enough without dice; just shout out a different number every couple of minutes.

You: "Okay, number two! Everybody ask some questions with 'Where!' Okay, now, number five! 'Who!'"

2) NUMBERS AND PRICES

LEVEL: Elementary to Intermediate

Review numbers by dictation or whatever. (That is, you say a number, and the students write it.)

Again, you can make this as easy or as complicated as you'd like; for intermediate students, you can do large numbers like 215,465 or 1,354,978.

Then you can have students practice in pairs by dictating numbers to each other.

Write some prices on the board in dollars, pounds, and Euros.

Board:

$385.49

You: "How do you say this price?"

Students: "Three-eight-five-forty-nine dollars."

You: "No, that's three HUNDRED and eighty-five dollars and forty-nine cents. About my salary, in other words."

Dorky Student: "But you get to travel."

You: "Yeah. All my dreams came true. Okay, now, do this with your partner. Student A – write a price. Ask, 'How do you say this price?' Student B, answer."

Board:

How do you say this price?

Or

What's this price?

(**Helpful Hint:** Numbers are as basic and important as anything and you can emphasize that to the students as they do this. Particularly to the rich kids who travel to other countries and buy a lot of shit.)

This activity by itself can serve as a warmer for the next activity:

3) PRICES AND FOOD

LEVEL: All

Have students review food vocabulary in pairs. (Your course book probably has pictures of food somewhere; have students look at the pictures in pairs and ask each other "What's this?" or "What are these?" or whatever. Get a fast food menu off the internet, if nothing else.)

If your student book doesn't have some kind of menu, it's not much trouble for you to write one:

Board:

Hamburger $2.99

Fish Sandwich $1.99

Fries (small) $.99

Fries (large) $1.50

Etc.

Demonstrate:

You: "How much is a hamburger?"

Fat Kid in the Front Row: "A hamburger is $2.99."

You: "Okay, now get in pairs and ask questions about the prices."

Board:

How much is a / an…?

(**Helpful Hint:** You might emphasize that the activity is just to practice the names and the numbers, and questions with "How much?" not to order food. That fabulous pleasure will have to wait.)

You: "How much is a kilogram of apples at (the local glitzy supermarket)?"

Rich Student: "Shit, that's for a woman to know!"

Hot Chick: "I don't know, but my mother's housecleaner might know. Should I call her?"

Board:

How much is…

a bottle of mineral water / Sprite / beer / wine / fruit juice

a kilogram of apples / potatoes / carrots / bananas / chicken / (etc.)

You: "Now get into pairs and see how many questions with 'How much?' your fevered imaginations can come up with."

Student: "What?"

You: "Get into pairs and ask your partner at least eight questions with 'How much?'"

See if your students have much knowledge of current prices! If you're teaching rich kids or rich housewives, this activity will probably sink quickly, as they won't know the prices of anything, so you can move right into activity number four.

4) LET'S TALK ABOUT YOUR AVARICE

LEVEL: Elementary to Intermediate

Students could review the "possessions" vocabulary. If your course book has a page with pictures of things and household objects, have the students review it. Or do it with balls, or lists, or the usual stuff.

Or elicit:

You: "Tell me some things you have with you now, in your pocket or in your bag."

Students: "Pencil! Latest expensive Apple product! A knife! A paperclip! A condom!"

Board:

Glasses

Pen

Watch

Mobile phone

Etc.

You: "What does this question mean?"

Board:

How much is…?

(To answer, rub your thumb and forefinger together in the universal sign for greed and penury.)

You: "Okay, get into pairs and ask questions with 'How much is your…?'"

Dorky Student: "How much is your watch?"

Rich Student: "Well, I don't know, what's the current price of gold?"

(**Helpful Hint:** If the students have studied the past tense form already, have them ask, "How much was your…?" which of course makes more sense.)

Dorky Student: "How much was your watch?"

Rich Student: "I took it off a business rival; he didn't need it anymore, if you understand me. He had kicked the time habit."

If, by some chance, your students are not rich, greedy dicks who love to talk about how much their stuff costs, you can make the question GENERAL. People are so greedy and acquisitive these days, they probably know a lot about that sort of shit.

Rich Student: "How much is a Microsoft Zune?"

Dorky Student: "Jesus Christ, who the hell knows? Ask me about Apple products!"

After that:

You: "Tell me some things that you have in your house."

Students: "TV, computer, car, sofa, chifforobe, Thai hooker."

(Board some of those things they say.)

You: "Okay, ask some more questions with 'How much?' about things in your house."

Rich Guy: "This is a wonderful topic. Let me discuss my IKEA furniture."

Hot Chick: "Can I discuss my Gucci bag again, even though it's not in my house?"

Let the students ramble on about their stuff for a while.

Board:

a plane ticket to Egypt (or some other place that is a popular tourist destination for your students).

You: "Tell me the names of some other places that are popular for holidays."

Students: "Thailand! Goa! Cyprus! Any place with cheap sex tourism!"

If you happen to work in a place where students aren't rich assholes, you can use "bus tickets" or "train tickets" to some nearby cities, instead of exotic holiday destinations.

Board:

How much is a plane ticket to…?

You: "Okay, now ask your partner four questions with 'How much is a plane ticket to…?'"

If the students enjoy all of this, you can get even more elaborate, and write the names of some different models of cars on the board, and they can ask each other "How much?" This will go over well with young men and rich guys:

Board:

How much is a new Toyota Corolla? Porsche Cayenne? Hyundai Sonata? (Etc.)

(**Helpful Hint:** Let them use the internet on their smartphones to look up the answers; they'll love it. Or you can look up the answers in advance and make photocopies or information gap worksheets with car prices, if you're feeling particularly inspired.)

5) JOBS AND PLACES / PRESENT SIMPLE WITH "DOES"

LEVEL: Elementary to Intermediate

First you need to review jobs.

If you have a course book, there are probably pictures of people in different jobs in it.

You: "Okay, get into pairs. Look at the pictures and ask, 'What's his / her job?'"

Or you can review jobs any of the usual ways.

Demonstrate:

You: "What's your job, Rich Guy?"

Rich Guy: "I'm a businessman."

You: "What's your job, Dorky Student?"

Dorky Student: "I'm an IT engineer, of course!"

You: "Okay, get up and move around the room – ask the other students, 'What's your job?'"

(Now, telling the students to get up and move around the room is one of those things they tell you to do all the time in course books and training classes – my experience is that in real life, students hate it and sometimes even refuse to do it, especially if you're teaching older people. So you could just have them ask the students next to them, in front of them, and behind them. They should get the point.)

If you're teaching high school kids or housewives, you could go with "What's your father's job?" or "What's your husband's job?"

Review vocabulary of places – if there are pictures of some different places in a city, have the students look at the pictures together and ask each other questions:

Student A: "What's this?"

Student B: "It's a hospital."

THEN it all comes swirling together in a fireball of glory.

Board:

Q: Where does a doctor work?

A: A doctor works in a hospital.

(Naturally this is a gross oversimplification, but much of Level One English is.)

Emphasize the S, which students always forget at the end of the verb. Draw a big S on the board. That's cute, right?

Then ask a student:

You: "Where does a teacher work?"

Student: "A teacher works in a crappy private language institute."

Erase the words "doctor" and "hospital" from your example so that you have:

Board:

Where does a _____ work?

A _____ works in a _____.

You: "Okay, now get into pairs – ask this question about different jobs."

You're reviewing jobs, places, AND present simple all in one swoop.

Good job, educator!

Now, you can make it more complicated for pre-intermediate and intermediate students.

You: "What does a teacher do?"

Student: "A teacher brings the light of knowledge into the world."

You: "Exactly. What does a businessman do?"

Rich Student: "A businessman eliminates the middle man."

You: "Uh…yeah."

Board:

What does a _____ do?

Where does a _____ work?

You: "Now get in pairs. Ask these two questions about different jobs."

(**Helpful Hint:** You could easily do this with advanced classes; just make the jobs more difficult.)

Student A: What does a claims adjuster do?

Student B: Claims adjusters investigate insurance claims by interviewing the claimant and witnesses, consulting police and hospital records, and inspecting property damage to determine the extent of the company's liability.

And you could add more questions for intermediate levels:

Board:

Would you like to be a…? Why / Why not?

Do you know anybody who is a / an…? Do they like their jobs?

What are the advantages and disadvantages of being a…?

6) COUNTRIES AND NATIONALITIES

LEVEL: Elementary to Intermediate

Have the students review countries.

Maybe your elementary course book has a map; maybe, probably, it connects this with the adjectives of nationality. ("Hi! I'm Jean-Paul! I'm from France! I'm French! I like bread!" Such stereotyping, shit.) Or you could get a map off the internet

You: "Okay, look at the map and point – ask this question."

(Now, obviously if you get a map off the internet, cover up the names before you photocopy it and hand it out.)

Board:

What's the name of this country?

Or of course, you can elicit: "Tell me 10 countries," or use the ball, or any of the other activities I keep yammering about.

So even very low-level students encounter questions with "What's your...?" pretty quickly:

You: "What's your nationality if you're from Spain?"

Hot Chick: "My nationality is Spanish." (A lot of students miss the point of the generic "you" and say, "I'm Spanish," even if they're not; that's okay for our purposes.)

(You'll probably have to elicit / translate / explain the meaning of "if" for very low-level classes.)

Board:

What's your nationality if you're from _____?

You: "Get in pairs and ask this question about different countries."

Now, suppose we want to add a few more complications.

Board:

What's the language / population / capital city of Spain?

You: "What are the answers to these questions?"

Students: (helpfully piping up)

"The language of Spain is Spanish."

"The population of Spain is 30,000,000."

"The capital city of Spain is Madrid."

You: "Okay, now get into pairs and ask these questions about DIFFERENT countries."

So it's a little geography quiz for them, in English! Like cross-training.

(**Helpful Hint:** Again, if you let them use their iPhones to find the answers, things will go a lot more smoothly. You could also emphasize that the answer "Sorry, I really don't know" is a perfectly normal part of everyday communication.)

7) NAMES / JOBS / NATIONALITIES

LEVEL: Elementary to Intermediate

Review vocabulary for jobs in pairs, and then nationalities in pairs. However you wish.

If you happen to have some celebrity magazines, like *PEOPLE* or *HELLO!* or whatever, this is a good use for them.

Give students magazines full of pictures of celebrities – or just a bunch of pictures of celebrities – and write:

Board:

What / name?

What / job?

Where / from?

You: "What are the correct forms of these questions for a man? For a woman?"

Students: (invariably chime in with the correct answers. Or not, and you give them the answers.)

You: "Now ask the questions in pairs, about the famous people here."

(**Helpful Hint:** Obviously, you want to find celebrities the students actually know something about, which might differ slightly country to country. Although everybody loves Lady Gaga.)

8) FAMILY

LEVEL: All

Review the vocabulary for people in families. You know the drill – use the picture dictionary, the book, the board, the ball, whatever.

If nothing else, draw your family tree, real or imagined on the board, and ask them who the people are, related to you.

You: "Okay, now ask questions about the family tree (or in the book or on the board or whatever)."

Board:

Who is…?

Student A: Who's Bill?

Student B: He's your uncle's special roommate.

For intermediate students, try the slightly more complicated:

Board:

What's _____'s _____'s name?

And demonstrate:

You: "What's Marie's husband's name?"

Hot Chick: "His name's Moneybags…I mean, his name is Andre."

Review the use of the apostrophe. And the "S" pronunciation. And the verb "to be," of course.

Then, you can have the students draw their own family trees and discuss them thusly.

Board:

What's your _____'s name?

How old is…?

Make it more complicated by reviewing jobs.

Board:

What's your _____'s job?

Dorky Student: "What's your mother's job?"

Hot Chick: "Well, of course she doesn't work, are you crazy?"

And there's a conversation about families, carefully constructed from jagged little pieces.

For upper-intermediate and advanced students, add more questions:

<u>Board:</u>

Where does _____ live?

What does _____ like doing in _____ free time?

What kind of car does _____ have?

What does he / she look like?

9) PLACING LOCATIONS AND GIVING DIRECTIONS

LEVEL: All

Again, if there is a map or some unit that offers some visual representation of directions, in your book, tell your students to focus on it.

Board:

Answer: It's on 2753 Paper Street, next to the abandoned factory.

You: "What's the question for this answer?"

Random Student: "Where is (our illustrious school)?"

Review prepositions of location – in a street (UK) on a street (US), by / near / next to / opposite.

You can do this easily enough by asking about people or things in the room.

You: "Where is Raoul?"

Random Student: "He's between Kumiko and Claudette. The perv."

(It shouldn't be TOO hard to establish that these terms can apply to buildings as well as people.)

You: "Where's the ancient battered CD player?"

Random Student: "In the chipped and ugly Formica cabinet!"

Write your local landmarks, such as they are, on the board:

Board:

McDonald's

The Holiday Inn Hotel

(Whatever) Nightclub

The (Whatever) Cinema

You: "Okay, now ask your partner 10 questions with 'Where is?' about this city."

Now, of course, you can use actual maps of the city, if you are so inclined.

As for "giving directions" – something most males understandably hate to do in real life, but for some reason don't mind doing in class –

Make yourself a little obstacle course of desks and chairs.

You: "How can I get to the front door of the class?"

Here, hilarity will erupt, no doubt, as they direct you to "turn right, go straight, turn left, go past" the chairs and desks.

After they finish crapping themselves with laughter:

Board:

How can I get to _____ from here?

You: "Okay, now ask your partner questions about these different places – how can I get to somewhere from here?"

(**Helpful Hint:** There are five million books with 20 million "information gap" maps, as mentioned; you can use one here if you like photocopies, extraneous pieces of paper, and confused students.

Now, my way? At least it's personal. Both of the students may know where something is, rendering this less-than-realistic conversation, but the fastest way to "realistic conversation" is open to debate. In any event, the lack of language gives the activity the challenge, not the geography.)

10) DATES

LEVEL: Beginner to Intermediate

Review the months of the year.

This is a good one for the ball. If your class is small enough to permit such frippery, throw the ball to one student, who says "January." He throws the ball to someone else, who says, "February." Another says, "March." And so on.

You'll have to knock the smiles off their faces with a goddamn shovel, I promise you.

Then do it backwards – December to January – and do it as many times as it takes to get it right.

Review the ordinal numbers "1st, 2nd, 3rd, 4th" with a ball, also. Same games.

Drill pronunciation of these, which will be fun because many nationalities can't manage the "th" sound. Have a laugh. You can board them in some form or another.

Or if you're feeling too hungover for that kind of stuff, just do it the usual way – write 'em on the board and drill pronunciation.

You: "What's the first month?"

Hot Chick: "January."

You: "What's the eighth month?"

Dorky Kid in the Back: "August."

Board:

What's the _____ month?

You: "Now ask your partner this question about some different months."

Do this for five minutes or so.

Board:

11/4/05

You: "How do we say this?"

(And ha ha, of course, it's different in Europe or America – it means November 4th in America and April 11th in Europe.)

You: "And what's the question for this answer?"

Dorky Student: "What's the date?"

You: "Write different dates on a piece of paper and ask your partner, 'What's the date?'"

After the students do that for a bit:

Board:

When's _____'s birthday?

You: "When's your birthday, Hot Chick?"

Hot Chick: "August eighth."

You: "Great, we're astrologically compatible. Will you be 18 soon?"

You could use this opportunity to review family:

Board:

When / mother / birthday?

You: "What's the correct form of this question?"

Random Student: "When's your mother's birthday?"

You: "Yeah, now ask some more questions about other family members. Who can tell me some more family members?"

Students: "Stepfather! Uncle's second wife! Baby mama! Illegitimate child!"

Board:

Father

Brother

Uncle

Grandmother

Etc.

You can do holidays:

You: "Who can tell me some holidays that are celebrated in America and Europe?"

Board:

Halloween

Christmas

Valentine's Day

New Year's Eve

International Woman's Day

International Sex Trafficking Awareness Day

Etc.

(**Helpful Hint:** Obviously if you're teaching Muslim or Chinese students, you have a whole different set of holidays and a different calendar. Good luck with that. But as always, if the students don't know something, that makes it all the more important to shove it down their throats, right?)

11) PRESENT SIMPLE FOOD ACTIVITY

LEVEL: All, but especially Pre-Intermediate to Intermediate

Let the students review the vocabulary pages about food and drink in pairs. Or just ask the students to name a bunch of different foods. Again you could use the ball.

Board:

Answer: I eat pizza twice a week.

You: "What's the question for this answer?"

Annoying Student: "How often do you eat pizza?"

Board:

How often do you eat pizza?

You: "Okay, what are some other things to say here?"

Point to "twice a week."

Students will hopefully describe a few different ways to express frequency. You can write:

Board:

Three times a year

Four times a month

Eight times a day

Some students will probably want to ask about "always" and "never" and "rarely" and "sometimes." Go into it if you must, but be sure to point out the proper placement of these words in a complete sentence – "I never eat chips."

Erase the "pizza" from the question and answer.

Board:

Do you like…?

How often do you eat…?

I eat _____ times a week.

You: "Get into pairs and ask your partner some questions about different foods."

(**Helpful Hint:** Often, you'll need to put some kind of arbitrary goal on this kind of thing. For example, "Ask you partner 10 questions" can be more productive than "Ask your partner some questions.")

You can demonstrate with students, first.

You: "Do you like cocktails?"

Hot Chick: "Of course."

You: "I bet you could tell me a few cock tales, baby. How often do you eat that...I mean, how often you drink cocktails?"

If you're of a mind to now review questions with DOES, and more stuff about family, you could board the following:

Board:

...mother like pizza?

How often / mother / pizza?

You: "Now ask your partner some questions about what foods your family eats."

12) PAST TENSE FOOD ACTIVITY

LEVEL: Pre-Intermediate to Advanced

<u>Board:</u>

I had bread and cheese for breakfast yesterday.

<u>You:</u> "What's the question for this answer?"

Fat Student: "What did you have for breakfast yesterday?"

Then you can erase the words "bread" "cheese" and "breakfast" from the board:

<u>Board:</u>

Q: What did you have for breakfast / lunch / dinner yesterday?

A: I had _____ for _____ yesterday

<u>You:</u> "Now get in pairs and ask your partners (five, 10, 20, whatever) questions about their meals yesterday."

Then do a few as a class – they could ask you about your meals, for example.

Student: "What did you have for dinner yesterday, Teacher?"

<u>You:</u> "Instant noodles with a can of tuna on top of it. And a lot of beer."

After they finish, write *"last Saturday / on your last birthday / January 1st / on the last big family holiday"* next to *"yesterday"* and have them ask some more questions.

13) BUYING FOOD ROLE PLAY

LEVEL: All

Give them some menus off the internet, or create one on the board, or use the menus from the student book, if they exist.

Draw stick figures on the board to indicate a fast-food restaurant clerk and a customer ordering fast food – use speech bubbles to elicit some possible questions from the clerk and some ways to order.

You: "What should the clerk say? What should the customer say?"

After discussing it briefly, you can write:

Board:

Typical questions:

"Can I take your order?"

"Anything else?"

"Would you like fries with that?"

Typical answers:

"A large coke and a cheeseburger, please."

(This can probably be done in English, albeit slowly and painfully, but you might translate a few of these, if you have some knowledge of your students' native language.)

You: "What does this mean in Xrusvenese?"

(If all the students agree, you know they probably understand it, even if you don't particularly know the translation.)

This may well lead to a lively discussion of possible variations on this theme. You could suggest that pointing at pictures on the wall is always an option.

If you're not feeling too hungover and embarrassed, you could demonstrate this by writing some prices for hamburgers, fries, sandwiches, and drinks on the board.

Board:

Hamburger $2.99

Cheeseburger $3.99

Chili Cheese Fries (small) $.99

Chili Cheese Fries (large) $1.99

And then stand behind your desk like the fast-food clerk you otherwise might have been, and might yet be:

You: "Welcome to Greasy's, may I take your order, please?"

You could use the CD player like a cash register, if you want to go for the Oscar.

After demonstrating:

You: "Okay, now – you four students be servers, and you students be customers."

You could even make paper hats for the servers; bringing in loads of ridiculous props and things might well fool the students into thinking they're doing a fun, realistic activity that is teaching them loads of English.

Although of course it might just be stupid and embarrassing to them. You gotta feel the room, you know?

Such nonsensical role plays are often surprisingly successful, though. I suppose they make you feel you're earning your money, if nothing else.

14) PERSONAL ITEMS

LEVEL: All

Review the vocabulary for possessions – computer, phone, car, watch, etc.

Board:

A: Yes, I have. I've got a mobile phone.

You: "What's the question?"

Random Student: "Have you got a mobile phone?"

Board:

A: I've got a Nokia mobile phone.

You: "And what's the question for this answer?"

Hot Chick: "'What kind of mobile phone have you got?' This is an important question, to my mind."

Make sure the students understand "What kind?" versus "What brand?"

Board:

A: It's in my pocket.

(Make sure students understand "pocket." Easy enough to point to your pocket, although discretion is advised.)

You: "What's the question?"

Dorky Student: "Where is your mobile phone?"

Most likely students have loads of electronic crap and will be happy to talk about it:

Board:

Have you got a / any…?

What kind of…have you got?

Where is it / are they now?

You might need to write some things on the board to move the conversation along, if there's not a list of them in your course book.

Board:

MP3 player

DVD player

Laptop computer

Car

Mistress

Most of these things are international words and won't need translating.

You: "Get into pairs. Ask your partner these questions about things that you have."

To make it more advanced, add a few more questions like:

Board:

What color

How often / use it

What / think of it?

15) PAST TENSE SMALL ITEM ACTIVITY

LEVEL: All

You can continue the above activity with the following, or do it as a follow-up activity on the next day.

Review personal items again – watch, pen, pencil, phone, computer, etc.

Board:

A: I bought this pen at (whatever local shop).

A: I bought this pen three days ago.

A: It was 15 (whatever local currency).

You: "What are the questions for these answers?"

Greedy Acquisitive Students: "Where did you buy your pen? When did you buy your pen? How much was it?"

Have students ask questions in pairs about the small things they have with them, and possibly about their items of clothing.

You: "Now ask your partner questions about some of their possessions."

Board:

Where did you buy your _____?

When did you buy your _____?

How much was it?

Rich Student 1: "How much was your girlfriend?"

Rich Student 2: "One trip to the Seychelles and a few bottles of champagne. Cheap at twice the price."

16) BORROWING SMALL PERSONAL ITEMS ROLE PLAY

LEVEL: Elementary to Intermediate

Demonstrate:

<u>You:</u> (speaking to a hot chick) "Excuse me, have you got a pencil?"

(Here there will undoubtedly be humorous confusion as she answers "Yes" or "Please" or whatever.)

<u>You:</u> "In English, 'Excuse me, have you got a pencil?' ACTUALLY means 'Can I have a pencil?' Or 'Give me a pencil, please.'"

<u>**Board:**</u>

"Excuse me, have you got a cigarette?"

"Yes, here you are." / "No, sorry."

Act it out with the hot chick, and then pretend not to give her the pencil back. Give the students 10 minutes or so to laugh, and then let them get a drink of water because they're choking on their own saliva.

After students recover from the oxygen depletion that excessive laughter has brought on, write the following:

<u>**Board:**</u>

Pen

Pencil

Piece of paper

Cigarette

Lighter

Match

Coin

<u>You:</u> "Now practice the dialogue – and actually hand the small items back and forth! Or of course, politely say 'No.'"

Again, using actual things here will make this feel like a realistic bit of communication, though of course it really isn't anything of the sort.

17) DRINKS

LEVEL: All

Review drinks vocabulary in the usual way.

Board:

A: Yes, I do.

A: I like red wine.

A: I drink red wine about twice a month.

You: "What are the questions for these answers, my little hedgehogs?"

Students: "'Do you like wine?' 'What kind of wine do you like?' and 'How often do you drink red wine?'"

Erase the word "wine" from the questions.

Board:

Do you like _____?

What kind of _____ do you like?

How often do you drink _____?

You: "Now ask your partner these three questions about different drinks."

Demonstrate:

You: "Do you like wine, Hot Chick?"

Hot Chick: "No. I only drink martinis. Or tequila. Or whatever is trendy."

(**Helpful Hint:** You might need to go through the pattern of answers with "once / twice / three times a day / month / year" and the students will probably also ask about "sometimes, always, rarely" and "never.")

Point out to the students that "What kind of wine do you like?" could be answered by "I like French wine" or "I like dry wine" or the name of a company, or even "I like expensive wine." They'll probably get the picture.

18) BUYING DRINKS ROLE PLAY

LEVEL: All

Here's another no-fuss yet usually successful role-playing activity that will, generally speaking, have the students deluded that they're learning something significant.

You could turn the classroom into a bar, coffee shop, or café – depending on whether alcohol is a crime punishable by death in your country of residence or not – and have some of the students be customers.

Board: (Draw a picture of a bartender, with a word balloon.)

"Can I help you?"

You: "A black coffee, please" or "A glass of beer, please."

Your book might have some example of this kind of dialogue; if not, you can use the board:

Board:

A: Can I help you?

B: A (glass of / cup of) _____, please.

A: Here you are. That's ($4.00) please.

Demonstrate:

You: "I'm the bartender. Hot Chick and Dorky Student, come up here and order some drinks from me."

Hot Chick: "A large martini, please. He's paying."

After serving them:

You: "Okay, now you students are bartenders, and the rest of you are customers. Put on your acting shoes and do some serious fucking role playing."

Remind them that feeling stupid probably means they're learning a lot.

19) PERSONAL INFORMATION

LEVEL: Elementary or First Day Activity for All Levels

<u>Board:</u>

Name?

Nationality?

Home City?

Job?

Address?

Mobile Phone Number?

Home Phone Number?

Married?

<u>You:</u> "What are the correct complete questions here?"

Dorky Student: "You should use 'What's your?' for all those questions. Except of course for 'Are you married?'"

<u>You:</u> "Okay, now – speak to your partner – ask all of these questions, and WRITE DOWN the answers."

Dorky Student: "Are you married, Hot Chick?"

Hot Chick: "Uh…no, that's not how I'd describe the arrangement, no."

<u>Board:</u>

How do you spell…?

<u>You:</u> "Remember that you are supposed to write the answers."

To stretch it out a bit:

<u>You:</u> "Now ask a different student the same questions."

So if you wanted to make this into some kind of ridiculous role play, you certainly can.

I like to call this the "Illegal Border Crossing Game."

You could turn the classroom into an Immigration office, for example, with some students being bureaucrats grilling them in Passport Control.

You: "We're going to play a game. You are spies, or illegal immigrants with fake documents. WRITE DOWN answers to all these questions on the board – but NOT the real information. WRITE IT DOWN IN YOUR FAKE PASSPORT. Write your secret identity here, not your real identity."

You'll probably have to demonstrate. Have one student do it, completing the fake passport with fake information.

Then, you play the Passport Control Officer. Take the fake passport, and ask the student questions, and see if they can remember what they wrote in the fake passport.

Once they see it demonstrated, they'll get the point.

Appoint some students to be Passport Control Storm Troopers, and others to be spies with fake documents, and play the game.

If they make a mistake – that is, they can't remember exactly what information they wrote in the fake passport – you can tell them they have to go to Guantanamo to be waterboarded and forced to simulate sex acts with other prisoners.

20) HOTEL CHECK-IN ROLE PLAY

Board:

HOTEL

(Draw a hotel clerk and front desk, if you can.)

Or you could stand there and act like one.

Board:

Good evening.

Reservation?

Last name?

First name?

Spell it.

Passport?

Credit card?

You: "What are the full questions when we check into a hotel?"

Students: "Have you got a reservation?" "What's your first name / last name?" "Can you spell it, please?" "Can I see your passport / credit card?"

Board:

Thank you.

Here's your key (card).

That's room 163.

You: "You students are receptionists, and you students are customers. Practice checking into a hotel."

(First demonstrate with the hot chick, and actually look at her passport and maybe see if she's really 18.)

(**Helpful Hint:** Again, you can make this a real role play easily enough, if that impresses your students. Use folded pieces of paper to represent passports, real credit cards, and real keys or key cards, and actually have the students hand them back and forth during the dialogue.)

You might put the customers with their backs to the board but let the receptionists look at the prompts on the board. Or vice versa.

You could expand the activity a bit:

Board:

When's breakfast / lunch / dinner?

When does the disco / restaurant / pool open / close?

Where's the elevator / sauna / gift shop / gym?

You: "Ask the clerk some questions about the hotel. Clerk – just make up some answers, you know. Whatever."

At your own discretion:

Board:

Where can I find hookers / men who'll buy me drinks / drugs in this city?

21) ASKING ABOUT FAVORITES AND PREFERENCES

LEVEL: All

Board:

What's your favorite color / food / car / sport / car / kind of phone?

You: "What does this word – 'favorite' – mean?"

Dorky Student: "That which we love more than all others."

You: "Right as always, Dork."

(You might need to review some general vocabulary with the ball or whatever, for lower-level classes, who might not easily think of different kinds of foods or sports.)

Demonstrate with a student:

You: "What's your favorite food?"

Hot Chick: "Sushi, of course."

You: "Don't you like hot sausage? I like eating peaches myself."

You could check pronunciation of some words related to movies and music and stuff, which might be similar in their native language but pronounced differently:

Board:

Jazz

Disco

Drum and Bass

You: "How do you pronounce this word?" (Point to different words.)

Students: "Drum and bass!"

You: "No, of course, BASS is a kind of fish! This word rhymes with face, as in off your face!" (Teacher laughs hysterically at his own joke, which no one else understands.)

Board:

What are your favorite kinds of music / books / movies?

What is your favorite song / book / movie?

You: "What's the difference between these questions?"

Dorky Student: (Will hopefully explain it to the class.)

Only do this if you are in a country where movies and music are not punishable by flogging, of course.

Board:

Who's your favorite actor / actress / singer / singing group?

WHY?

I like _____ because he / she / they _____ .

Let students discuss these questions and answers for a while, then do a few as a class.

You: "Who's your favorite singer, Hot Chick? Anybody want to bet me $50 that it's Lady Gaga?"

Hot Chick: "No, I like rap and hip hop because they always sing about money."

22) GIVE ME YOUR STUPID OPINIONS

Board:

Good

OK

Bad

You: "What are some words that mean the same thing as 'good'? 'Bad'? 'OK'?"

Students: "Terrible, awful, shitty, lame-ass, great, wonderful, not bad, so-so, etc."

(You can write some on the board and discuss them.)

Board:

What do you think of...?

You: "What do you think of Lady Gaga?"

Dorky Student: "Her nudity distracts one from her large nose."

Hot Chick: "She's a brilliant role model for 12-year-olds. Do you like her, Teacher?"

You: "I haven't willingly listened to music since that guy from Nirvana killed himself. What do you think of Apple iPhones?"

Dorky Student: "I think they're fucking awesome but I disapprove of their Chinese sweatshops."

Rich Guy: "Hey, sweatshop owners have to eat too!"

Board:

I think he / she is...

You: "Ask your partner ten (20, 30) questions with 'What do you think of...'"

Let the students discuss their opinions of various things – if they can't think of any examples.

Board:

English people / Japanese food / tequila / Harry Potter / cats / George W. Bush / French food / bananas / Snickers bars / David Beckham / whatever other things are popular and well-known to your dimmest students

(**Helpful Hint:** You could also use this to practice object pronouns – "I like / don't like him /her / it / them.")

23) SPORTS / ACTIVITIES

LEVEL: Pre-Intermediate to Advanced

Review vocabulary of sports in the lively way of your choice.

Board:

A: Yes, I can. I can play tennis.

A: I play tennis about twice a week.

A: I play tennis at the local court.

A: I play after work on Fridays.

A: I play with my cousin.

You: "What are the questions for these answers?"

Students: "Can you play tennis?" "How often do you play?" "Where do you play tennis?" "When do you play tennis?" "Who do you play with?"

You: "Correct. You never cease to please me with your perspicacity, my little hedgehogs. Now get into pairs – ask your partner 10 questions about sports."

Student: "Teacher, what's a hedgehog?"

You: "We'll talk about that next lesson."

Board:

Can you play _____?

How often do you play _____?

Where do you play _____?

When do you play _____?

Who do you play with?

(**Helpful Hint:** You might emphasize here that you are trying to get students to produce English sentences, not to tell the complete and detailed truth about their lives. Encourage them to make up some answers if they're cubicle-bound office workers.)

24) PAST TENSE SPORTS ACTIVITY

Review some vocabulary of sports, and board them or whatever.

You: "What's the past tense of 'play'?"

Students: "Played!"

You: "What's the past tense of 'is'?"

Students: "Was!"

You: "I've never been as happy as I am right now."

Board:

A: The last time I played baseball was in 2005.

You: "What's the question for this answer?"

Dorky Student: "When was the last time you played baseball?"

(Helpful Hint: You'll probably have to go through time expressions like "three weeks ago," "eight days ago," "when I was a child," etc. And of course, "I have never played those sports, I, like most modern youths, sit indoors in front of the computer all day.")

Board:

I played baseball at my school.

I played baseball with my friends.

You: "And what are the questions here?"

Dorky Student: "Where did you play baseball? Who did you play baseball with?"

Board:

When was the last time you played _____?

Where did you play _____?

Who did you play _____ with?

You: "Get into pairs and ask your partner these questions about 10 different sports."

25) TIME AND PRESENT SIMPLE DAILY ACTIVITIES

LEVEL: All, especially Pre-Intermediate to Intermediate

Review vocabulary of things we do every day.

If there's nothing like a list of these activities in the book, ask:

You: "Tell me some things that people do every day."

Student 1: "Get up!"

Student 2: "Drink coffee!"

Dorky Student: "Study English!"

Hot Chick: "Eat sushi and drink martinis!"

Rich Guy: "Bang my mistress!"

You: "Excellent, little hedgehogs. VERY good. Gold stars for everybody."

Board:

Get up

Go to work / school

Have breakfast / lunch / dinner

Go home

Take a shower

Go to sleep

Review time – use a clock in the classroom, or from the book, or draw a few clocks (or digital timers, of course) on the board.

Board:

9:30

You: "What time is it?"

Student: "It's nine-thirty. Or half-past-nine."

You: "Wrong. It's time for me to get a watch!" (Teacher laughs at his own joke while a few students smile politely.)

(**Helpful Hint:** It's up to you whether you want to get into all that "quarter past" and "quarter to" stuff, and you might be surprised how weak students are at saying time. It's relatively important and rather difficult in English. For lower-level students, budget an extra 10 minutes just for practicing time, via dictation and pairwork.)

Board:

A: I usually get up at 8:30 am.

You: "What's the question here?"

Dorky Student: "What time do you usually get up?"

Board:

What time do you usually _____ ?

You: "Okay, (indicate the daily activities) ask your partner at least seven questions about things they do every day."

If you want to expand this and practice other forms of present simple, you could do the following:

Board:

A: My mother gets up at 8:00 am.

You: "Now what's THIS question? Notice that S, baby!"

Dorky Student produces the correct answer, as usual.

Board:

What time does your mother / father / brother / Thai hooker get up?

You: "Ask your partner 10 questions about what time your family does various things. Or your mistress, or rich sponsor, or whatever."

26) PAST TENSE DAILY ACTIVITIES

LEVEL: Pre-Intermediate to Advanced

Board:

What time do you get up?

You: "What's the answer to this?"

Hot Chick: "I get up early to go to Pilates class. Unless I have a bad hangover."

Board:

I get up at 7.00 am.

You: "How do we change this question and answer to the past tense?"

Students: "What time did you get up yesterday?" "I GOT up at 7.00 am."

Board: (erase "do")

What time did you _____ yesterday?

I _____ at 7.00 am.

You: "What's the past tense of 'get'?"

Students: "Got!"

You: "Okay – Hot Chick – what time did you get up yesterday?"

Hot Chick: "I got up at 10.30 am yesterday."

You: "Never mind that, what did you sleep in yesterday? Just your panties?"

Refer the students to vocabulary of things we do every day.

You: "What's the past tense of 'get' up? 'Have' lunch? 'Go' to sleep?"

Students: "Got up! Had lunch! Went to sleep!"

You: "I'm feeling pure bliss now. Okay – now ask your partner 10 questions with 'What time did you...yesterday?'"

(**Helpful Hint:** You can add other times, of course – the day before yesterday, on your last birthday, on January 1st, whatever.)

27) FUTURE TENSE DAILY ACTIVITIES

Once again, review the verbs for things that we do every day and maybe times, if need be.

Board:

What time...get up tomorrow?

You: "What's the question here?"

Dorky Student: "What time are you going to get up tomorrow?"

You: "You make the sunshine seem as dark as the Mariana Trench, kid."

Board:

What time are you going to...tomorrow?

You: "What time are you going to get up tomorrow, Hot Chick?"

Hot Chick: "When I feel like it – whenever my champagne hangover wears off."

You: "What time are you going to go to bed tomorrow?"

Hot Chick: "Well, that won't be my choice, exactly..."

You might review time here again, depending.

Board:

I'm not sure / I don't have any plans / It depends

You: "What do these phrases mean?"

Students: (chattering like a flock of drunken magpies; eventually someone produces the correct answer.)

You: "Right! Okay, now ask your partner 10 questions about your day tomorrow. Remember, it's okay to say, 'I don't know yet.'"

Board:

Are you going to...tomorrow?

You: "Okay, what are some things that we do SOMETIMES? Not every day, but sometimes?"

Dorky Student: "Talk to girls!"

Rich Guy: "See our families!"

Hot Chick: "Think!"

<u>Board:</u>

Watch TV / play computer games / see your friends / eat fast food / etc.

<u>You:</u> "Now ask your partner some questions with 'Are you going to…?'"

28) FUTURE PLANS

LEVEL: Intermediate to Advanced

<u>You:</u> "How do we usually ask about future plans in English?"

Students: "Will!"

<u>You:</u> (deep weary sigh) "Uh, no, not really…"

Dorky Student: "'Going to,' of course, Teacher!"

<u>You:</u> "Yeah, let's go with that for the moment."

Students: "Why can't we use 'will,' Teacher?"

<u>You:</u> "Uh…next lesson. Or, uh, maybe Dorky Kid wants to explain that?"

Dorky Student: "Next lesson, Teacher."

<u>Board:</u>

What are you going to do next weekend? / on your next holiday? / on your next birthday? / December 31st? / next summer?

(**Helpful Hint:** Remind students that "I don't have any plans" is a perfectly acceptable answer to this question.)

<u>You:</u> "What are you going to do tonight, Hot Chick?"

Hot Chick: (twirling hair in her fingers and smiling coyly) "Oh, well, I don't have any plans…"

<u>You:</u> "Okay, now get into pairs and ask 10 questions with 'going to.'"

(For upper-intermediate students, you could review / introduce the concept of "might" here.)

<u>You:</u> "I might try to nail the hot chick tonight, or I might just get drunk with my friends."

Have students practice in pairs and then ask you a few questions about your life.

29) PRESENT CONTINUOUS

LEVEL: Pre-Intermediate to Intermediate

You could begin by reviewing all the verbs that the students know – free time activities, etc. Use the ball or ask each student to name a verb and write some or all of them on the board.

Board:

A: I work.

A: I'm working.

You: "What's the difference between these questions?"

Students: (all kinds of wrong or partially correct stuff)

You: "Not quite…what times are we talking about, here?"

Dorky Student: "Well, of course, the first question talks about every day and the second question talks about right now."

You: "Right-o! Now, what are the questions for these two answers?"

Dorky Student: "'What do you do?' and 'What are you doing?'"

You: "Okay, class, what are you doing?"

Students: "We're studying English!"

You: "Exemplary. What are you doing now, Hot Chick?"

Hot Chick: "I'm just sitting here in my tight pants."

You: "Good! And what are you doing, Lazy Student?"

Lazy Student: "Playing ANGRY BIRDS. Man, that shit is fun!"

You: "Right. Now – how can we change the question 'What are you doing?' to talk about he or she?"

Dorky Student: "'What's he doing?' Or, 'What's she doing?'"

You: "Fine. What's Hot Chick doing now, class?"

Students: "She's just sitting there being hot."

You: "Ah, but also aging quickly, don't forget about that."

Now – you'll need pictures here – usually the student book will have plenty of pictures on various pages – or you can bring in magazine pictures or pictures of people on the internet doing random shit.

You: "Open your books to some random pages – ask your partner, 'What's he doing? What's she doing? What are they doing?'"

Demonstrate with a few pictures chosen at random from the book. Course books are usually filled with plenty of pictures of multicultural groups of students doing different wholesome activities.

You: (showing picture from book) "What's he doing?"

Rich Student: "He's washing the dishes...what happened? Did he lose his penis in an accident?"

You: "That's certainly one possible explanation. Now ask your partner 10 questions about the pictures."

30) PRESENT CONTINUOUS / CLOTHES

LEVEL: All

Review vocabulary of clothes as you wish.

Board:

wear

You: "Class, what's Hot Chick wearing?"

Students: "Oh, tight pants and a leopard-print top with her bra showing, as usual!"

You: "Excellent. But – complete sentences."

Students: "She's wearing tight pants."

You: "Good! Not for much longer, hopefully!"

Board:

Her bra straps are black.

You: "What's the question for this answer?"

Dorky Student: "What color are her bra straps?"

You: "Excellent."

Board:

What's he / she wearing?

What color is it?

What color are they?

Now – you could do this just talking about people in class, but it's probably better to use pictures of people, to avoid any kind of snooty criticisms and snobbish class conflict.

Most likely, there are plenty of color photos of happy multicultural groups of people in your course books. Use these or bring in pictures off the internet or from fashion magazines.

You: "What's he wearing?"

Students: "He's wearing a Dolce & Gabbana hooded fleece ($300)."

You: "Okay, get into pairs – find different pictures of people in (your course books) and ask these two questions."

If you're using celebrity magazines you could expand the activity to include these questions:

Board:

What's his / her name?

What does he / she do?

What's he / she doing?

Or, if you are using a fashion magazine, and want more advanced questions:

Board:

Where was this made?

Who designed it? / What company made this?

What material is it made from?

How much does it cost?

31) FURNITURE AND FLATS

LEVEL: Pre-Intermediate to Intermediate

Review vocabulary of furniture and apartments.

Board:

Is there a / an…in this room?

You: "Can anybody explain / translate this idea?"

Dorky Student: (explains the point in profound and exciting detail)

Board:

Yes, there is.

No, there isn't.

You: "Is there a battered ancient CD player in this room?"

Students: "Yes, there is!"

You: "Is there a modern interactive whiteboard in this room?"

Students: "No, there isn't!"

You: "Now we're cooking with gas."

Board:

A: It's on the shelf next to a pile of leftover photocopies.

A: It's a Panasonic.

You: "What are the questions for these answers?"

Students: "Where's the CD player? What kind of CD player is it?"

You: "Fine. Okay, now ask your partner five questions about this room with 'Is there…?'"

Then erase "in this room" and write "in your flat."

Board:

There are four televisions in my flat.

You: "What's the question?"

Rich Student: "How many televisions are there in your flat? But that's not enough. Don't you have one in the bathroom?"

Board:

How many _____ are there in your flat?

You: "How can we change the question 'Where is the CD player?' and 'What kind is it?' to the plural?"

Dorky Student: "Where are they? What kind are they?"

You: "Okay, now ask your partner 10 questions about their house, or this room, with 'Are there any…?'"

(If students finish quickly, unable to think of enough questions about a flat, you might prompt them with some vocabulary to put in the gaps.)

Board:

Doors

Windows

Sofas

Chairs

Shelves

Computers

Telephones

Empty bottles of hard liquor

Dead hookers

Etc.

For more advanced classes you could add more questions:

(**Helpful Hint:** You could have them draw maps of their apartments, if you happen to think that such an invasion of privacy would go over well in your class.)

Or, you could have students look at pictures of rooms and houses in the book and ask the questions.

Add a spurious game element by having one student look at pictures of a room for one minute, then cover the picture and try to remember while another student asks questions.

You could also have students draw the house or room that a student is describing; however, in my experience, this will just get a lot of students screaming that they can't draw and that this isn't art class, etc.

32) PAST TENSE VERBS

LEVEL: Pre-Intermediate to Intermediate

Go through the list of regular and irregular verbs that the students have studied. Probably best to do this as a quick drill.

You: "What's the past tense of 'get laid'?"

Students: "Got laid."

You: "What's the past tense of 'take a pill'?"

Students: "Took a pill."

Board:

What's the past tense of . . .?

You: "Now – books closed – get into pairs, and ask your partner 10 questions: 'What's the past tense of different verbs?'"

33) PAST TENSE ACTIVITIES

LEVEL: All

<u>**Board:**</u>

What…you do last Friday / Saturday / Sunday?

<u>**You:**</u> "What's the missing word here?"

Keen Student: "Did!"

<u>**You:**</u> "What did you do last night, Hot Chick?"

Hot Chick: "I drank champagne and got laid in the back of my father's Mercedes."

<u>**You:**</u> "Fine. Okay, now get in pairs and ask at least 10 past tense questions about last Friday, Saturday, and Sunday."

(This is particularly important: Tell them they need to ask 10 questions here, otherwise you'll just get "Nothing special" or "I watched TV" and then they're back to playing ANGRY BIRDS.)

You'll probably need to prompt them a bit:

<u>**Board:**</u>

What time did you…?

Where did you…?

Who did you…with?

If you want to continue it a bit, you can erase "last Saturday and Sunday" and write some other times:

<u>**Board:**</u>

What did you do…

on your last birthday?

on your last holiday?

on your mother's last birthday?

after class yesterday?

on Christmas day last year?

Etc.

Choose appropriate holidays and such.

34) FUTURE TENSE USAGE OF PRESENT CONTINUOUS

LEVEL: Intermediate

<u>Board:</u>

I'm having dinner now.

I'm having dinner with my mother tonight at 8:00.

<u>You:</u> "What's the difference between these two questions?"

Students: (a bunch of wrong random shit)

<u>You:</u> "No. You see, in the second question, we are using present continuous to talk about DEFINITE ARRANGED PLANS in the near future."

(**Helpful Hint:** Emphasize this again. It's a hard sell.)

<u>You:</u> "What's the question for these two answers?"

Students: "'What are you doing now?' and 'What are you doing tonight at 8:00?'"

<u>You:</u> "Okay, now get into pairs – ask your partner, 'What are you doing tonight?'"

But the problem is, they won't have any definite plans, for the most part.

And to emphasize that this is used for definite plans in the future, especially involving people, you need diaries.

You could try to have students write diaries – but in fact, most of them won't have the imagination for it.

So you could prepare "Diary A" and "Diary B" – with a lot of entries like "lunch with Steven Spielberg" and "skiing with George Bush Jr." (See Rock Star Schedules in Part Three.)

Students could ask about each other's diaries.

Or, you could do it on the board without photocopying anything:

<u>Board:</u>

MONDAY

TUESDAY

WEDNESDAY

THURSDAY

FRIDAY

SATURDAY

SUNDAY

(Make a grid with spaces for times and meetings.)

You: "Okay, now, tell me a famous person for Monday."

Students: "Lady Gaga!"

You: "Now tell me an activity."

Students: "Have dinner!"

Board:

Monday – Dinner with Lady Gaga, 8:30 pm

(Repeat for each day of the week, with a new celebrity – you can schedule something for morning, afternoon, and evening if you want the activity to go on for a while.)

You: "Okay, this is Steven Spielberg's (or whatever famous person's) diary for the week. What's he doing on Monday?"

Students: "Dinner with Lady Gaga! 8:30 pm!"

You: "Complete sentences, you little scamps."

Students: "Steven Spielberg is having dinner with Lady Gaga at 8.30 pm!"

You: "I'm getting all tingly. Excellent."

Dorky Student: "Teacher, can we use 'going to'?"

You: (deep weary sigh) "Yes. No. I don't know. Whatever. Okay, now ask your partner some questions – what is Steven Spielberg doing on Tuesday, Wednesday, etc."

35) ARE VS. DO

LEVEL: Elementary to Intermediate

<u>Board:</u>

_____ *you from France?*

_____ *you like cats?*

<u>You:</u> "What are the correct words to compete these sentences?"

<u>Dorky Student:</u> "ARE you from France? DO you like cats?"

<u>You:</u> "Okay, now WHY?"

<u>Students:</u> (confused, agitated babbling)

<u>You:</u> (finally) "Because we use ARE with questions with nouns or adjectives, and DO with questions about actions — with verbs."

<u>Board:</u>

_____ *she a teacher?*

_____ *he have a car?*

_____ *they teachers?*

<u>You:</u> "And what are the correct words for THESE spaces?"

<u>Students:</u> "Is / does / are!"

<u>You:</u> "Correct. NOW, get in pairs. Ask your partner five questions with DO, five questions with DOES, five questions with IS, five questions with ARE! Do it now! Make it so!"

(**Helpful Hint:** You can use dice here, if they are handy.)

<u>Board:</u>

1-2) Are

3) Is

4-5) Do

6) Does

You: "Okay, now roll the dice and make questions for your partner."

Demonstrate:

After rolling a 4:

You: "Hot Chick…do you think it's HOT in here?"

Hot Chick: "Oh yes, Teacher, I think it's VERY hot in here."

36) PAST TENSE HOLIDAY ACTIVITY

LEVEL: Intermediate to Advanced

<u>**Board:**</u>

HOLIDAY

DAY OFF

WEEKEND

<u>**You:**</u> "What's the difference between these words?"

Students: (confused babbling before someone eventually explains it)

<u>**You:**</u> "Who can tell me some things people do on holiday?"

Student 1: "Swim!"

Student 2: "Use a lot of plastic bottles!"

Student 3: "Do sex tourism!"

<u>**Board:**</u>

What…do on your last holiday?

<u>**You:**</u> "And what's the magic missing word here?"

Students: "DID!"

<u>**Board:**</u>

Where…go?

Who…with?

Where…stay?

What…think of the food / hotel / people?

What…do during the day / the evening?

…buy anything?

…go to any nightclubs?

…become engaged to any local residents?

You: "Okay, what are the correct questions here?"

Students: (blabber for a while, and eventually come up with the correct answers)

You: "Now ask your partner at least 10 questions about the last time they traveled to a different country. Or, you know, different city, if you're talking to a poor person."

37) MORE DICE QUESTIONS

LEVEL: Intermediate to Advanced

Board:

1) What do you think of _____?

2) How often do you _____?

3) Where do you usually _____?

4) What / Who is your favorite _____?

5) Can you _____?

6) Are there _____? / Is there _____?

Demonstrate – roll a 3.

You: "Hot Chick, where do you usually meet rich guys?"

Hot Chick: "Well, there are plenty of rich guys desperate for good-looking young chicks in Germany, for example."

You: "Good! Okay, roll the dice and complete questions for your partner to answer."

38) ADDITIONAL DICE QUESTIONS

LEVEL: Intermediate to Advanced

<u>**Board:**</u>

1) Do you like _____?

2) How much _____? / How many _____?

3) Have you got _____?

4) What kind _____?

5) Where is _____? / Are _____?

6) What color _____?

<u>**You:**</u> "Okay, roll the dice, make a question for your partner, and don't bug me too much while you do it!"

39) THE DICE GAME TO END ALL DICE GAMES

LEVEL: Intermediate to Advanced

<u>Board:</u>

1)

2)

3)

4)

5)

6)

<u>You:</u> "Okay, tell me a topic."

Students: (some confusion)

<u>You:</u> "A topic. Something to talk about. A theme."

Dorky Student: "Uh…computers."

<u>You:</u> "Fine."

<u>Board:</u>

1) COMPUTERS

<u>You:</u> "Okay, another?"

Hot Chick: "Uh…feminism?"

Students: (general hilarity erupts)

<u>Board:</u>

1) COMPUTERS

2) FEMINISM

And so on, until you have six topics.

<u>You:</u> "Okay, now roll the dice, and ask your partner AT LEAST five (or 10 or whatever) questions about that topic. Any tense you want."

The beauty about this one is that if the topics are boring, the students will blame each other, and not you.

40) USING ALL THE TENSES TOGETHER

LEVEL: Intermediate to Upper-Intermediate

<u>Board:</u>

What time _____ you get up?

<u>You:</u> "Okay, how do we complete this question for the present tense?"

Students: "Do!"

<u>You:</u> "Sublime. And for the past tense?"

Students: "Did!"

<u>You:</u> "And for the future?"

Students: "Will!"

<u>You:</u> "Ah, not really, but for the purposes of this activity, let's go with it."

<u>Board:</u>

What time do you usually get up?

What time did you get up yesterday?

What time will you get up tomorrow?

<u>You:</u> "Remember? What's the past tense of 'get up'?"

Students: "GOT UP!"

<u>You:</u> "Okay, ask your partner a question in the past, present, and future."

(**Helpful Hint:** Then you can change the verb to "go to bed, go to class, have lunch, have dinner," etc., and have them ask three questions with each verb in the past, present, and future.)

41) MORE COMBINATION WORK

LEVEL: Intermediate to Advanced

<u>Board:</u>

What do you usually do in the evenings?

<u>You:</u> "How can I change this to the past tense?"

Dorky Student: "What did you do yesterday evening?"

<u>You:</u> "Superb. And the future?"

Students: "What are you going to do tomorrow evening?"

<u>You:</u> "Fine. Now, ask those three questions to your partners!"

<u>Board:</u>

What did you do…?

What do you usually do…?

What are you going to do…?

(after the students blather away happily for awhile)

<u>You:</u> "Now – different times! Ask your partners questions in each tense until your fucking gums bleed, you little sweethearts."

<u>Board:</u>

On Saturdays / last Saturday / next Saturday

On Christmas / last Christmas / next Christmas

On your summer vacation / last summer vacation / next summer vacation

(Naturally, be sensitive: don't use Christmas if you are teaching Chinese or Muslim students; try to find the date or name of one of their weird heathen celebrations and use that instead.)

42) TEN QUESTION CHALLENGE

LEVEL: Intermediate to Advanced

Basically this is a dice game without the dice.

You: "Okay, somebody give me a topic."

Dorky Student: "Computers."

Rich Guy: "Tax-deferred annuities."

You: "Okay, let's go with computers. The challenge: each student must ask 10 questions to their partner about computers."

Or you could do it with different topics, stuff you studied already.

You: "Okay, what did we study yesterday?"

Keen Student: "Past tense. And we read a text about Bill Gates."

You: "Okay – the challenge: ask your partner 10 questions in the past tense."

Dorky Student: "About Bill Gates?"

You: "Uh…yeah! Good idea! Ten questions about Bill Gates! In the past!"

(We can see that the difference between a professional and an incompetent amateur is the ability to improvise and bullshit.)

For lower levels, you could make it a "Five Question Challenge."

You: "Okay – ask your partner five questions with 'What' (or 'How many,' or 'How much,' or whatever.)"

43) PRESENT PERFECTION ONE

You: "Tell me some cities."

Students: "Dubai! Moscow! Guatemala City! East Lansing! Vodkaberg!"

Board: (as the students shout them out)

Dubai

Moscow

(Etc.)

(**Helpful Hint:** Now, hopefully the students will shout out the names of cities that are nearby and cities that they visit often. If not, use your undoubtedly extensive knowledge of their culture and country to write some cities that are suitable, and that the students actually have visited.)

You: "How do we make questions in the present perfect tense?"

Students: "Have or has plus the third form!"

You: "Affirmative. What's the third form of 'be'?"

Students: "Been."

Board:

Have you been to....? (preferably, write this to the left of the cities, so you get)

Have you been to Dubai?

Have you been to Moscow?

(Etc.)

You: "What's ANOTHER question we can ask in present perfect?"

Students: (plenty of horrified confused babbling)

You: "Okay, try this one."

Board:

How many times have you been to...? (Again, board this to the left of the cities.)

You: "Ask these two questions about all the cities on the board."

Demonstrate:

You: "Have you been to Dubai, Hot Chick?"

Hot Chick: "Yes, I have."

You: "How many rich guys have taken you to Dubai, Hot Chick?"

Hot Chick: "More than a few. But never quite enough for my tastes."

44) PRESENT PERFECTION

LEVEL: Upper-Intermediate to Advanced

This is one of those bitch-kitty grammar points that most teachers hate. Gotta be patient and methodical.

You: "What's the third form of 'visit?'"

Students: "Visited. Same-same past tense."

You: "Yes. What's the third form of 'see'?"

Students: "Seen."

You: "What's the third form of 'eat'?"

Students: "Eaten."

Board:

Have you ever eaten / seen / played…?

You: "Okay – ask about five different foods, five different animals, and five different games. You heard me! Step up!"

Demonstrate:

You: "Have you ever eaten at McDonald's, Fat Kid?"

Fat Student: "Yes, I have."

You: "Have you ever seen a pig?"

Fat Student: "Yes, I have. On many a plate with a side order of rice."

You: "I've seen more pigs in American nightclubs than I care to talk about. Have you ever played tennis?"

Fat Student: "On Xbox, you mean?"

And of course you can contrast the activity with the past tense:

Board:

When did you…?

Where did you…?

Why did you…?

Demonstrate:

You: "So, Hot Chick, have you ever eaten sushi?"

Hot Chick: "Yes, I have. I have eaten sushi many times."

You: "When did you last eat sushi?"

Hot Chick: "Last night, with you."

You: "That's right. And how much did it cost?"

Hot Chick: "Well, judging from the expression on your face when the bill came, quite a lot."

You: "Definitely. 'Kay, class – why was the FIRST question in the present perfect, and the SECOND and THIRD questions in the past tense?"

Dorky Student: "The first question was general, not about any specific time. The second and third questions were about specific times."

You: "Exactly. You pounced on that grammar like a puma, son. Good job. Okay, everybody – ask your partner 10 questions in the present perfect! And if they say yes, ask TWO MORE questions in the past simple."

45) PAST CONTINUOUS

LEVEL: Pre-Intermediate to Intermediate

<u>**Board:**</u>

Where are you?

What are you doing?

<u>**You:**</u> "Class, where are we?"

Students: "We are in English class. In our grimy industrial city."

<u>**You:**</u> "And what are we doing?"

Students: "We are studying English with our brilliant and benevolent teacher."

<u>**You:**</u> "Exactly. Now, how do we change that to the past tense?"

Students: "Where were you? What were you doing?"

<u>**You:**</u> "Now, what tense is this?" (Indicate the second sentence.)

Dorky Student: "Past progressive?"

Keen Student: "No, past continuous!"

<u>**You:**</u> "Aha – in fact, they are one and the same. Now…"

<u>**Board:**</u>

I studied.

I was studying.

<u>**You:**</u> "What's the difference between these two sentences?"

Students: (horrified explosion of raucous voices; some students begin to cry.)

<u>**You:**</u> "Relax. It's not that difficult. The first sentence, 'I studied' – means it finished in the past. The second sentence, I was studying – means it WASN'T FINISHED IN THE PAST. Finished now, perhaps, but at some time in the past, it was IN PROGRESS."

Students: (tears of horror turn to tears of joy)

You: "So, to use past continuous, we need to talk about a very narrow period of time in the past."

Board:

Where were you and what were you doing yesterday at…

6:30 am? 8:15 am? 9:45 am? 11:55 am? 3:15 pm? 6:30 pm? 9:10 pm? 11:45 pm?

You: "Remember – the first question – 'Where were you?' – is about the PLACE. The second question is about an ACTION IN PROGRESS IN THE PAST."

Demonstrate:

You: "Where were you yesterday at 9.10 pm, Rich Guy?"

Rich Guy: "I was at the home of a business rival."

You: "And what were you doing?"

Rich Guy: "I decline to answer that question on the grounds that it might incriminate me."

You: "Wow, fancy English. Where were you at 3:15 pm?"

Rich Guy: "I was at the gym."

You: "What were you doing?"

Rich Guy: "I was waiting for my bodyguards to finish exercising."

46) TRIUMPH OF THE WILL

LEVEL: Intermediate to Advanced

Board:

I _____ go to work tomorrow at 8:00 am.

You: "How do we fill in this blank?"

Students: "WILL!"

You: "WRONG! WRONG! WRONG!"

Dorky Student: "As we remember, GOING TO is for future plans."

You: "Yes…so when do we use 'will'? What does 'will' mean?"

Students: (confused wailing)

You: "Okay – think of it this way – 'will' is usually for a NEW IDEA about the future. For example, 'Ah, the phone is ringing. I'll answer this.' (Demonstrate with your phone – they will be shocked and awed.) It's used most often in conversation thusly…"

Board:

Do you think you will ever…

be rich? visit China? own your own business? be famous? own a Mercedes?

(The trick here is finding things that your students haven't already done en masse; Rich Guy, obviously, isn't going to have much to say here.)

Board:

Do you think there will ever be…

a female president of your country? a nuclear war? a snowstorm in the middle of June? a time when there is zero percent unemployment? people living on Mars?

When do you think you will…

get married? retire? buy your first house? (etc.)

And you should go through the answers with the students, probably just by boarding them:

Board:

I hope so. / I hope not.

I really don't know.

I think so. / I don't think so.

(**Helpful Hint:** This activity requires a fair bit of knowledge of your students and their country, in order to come up with relevant questions. And thus might well just be skipped. But students are often surprisingly insistent about forcing you to explain "will.")

47) THE CONDITION MY CONDITION IS IN

LEVEL: Intermediate to Advanced

This grammar point is the second conditional. What would you do if...? If + past tense, and would + infinitive, for all you grammar buffs out there. This grammar point is used to describe an unreal or unlikely hypothetical situation.

For some reason, most text books are fond of offering nothing much other than the following for the conversation portion of this lesson:

"What would you do if you won $1,000,000 in the lottery? Discuss with your partner."

Ostensibly not a bad thing to talk about, but it will basically get you nothing other than this:

"Well, I guess I'd buy a nice car and maybe a house, and probably I'd take a long holiday and travel around the world, but I'd save about half of it and give some to my family."

Okay. Conversation finished. That took, what, maybe a minute?

Then the book might say something like: "Ask your partner a few questions in the second conditional! What would you do if...?"

Basically, it is a bad idea to assume your students have any imagination whatsoever.

So try the following:

Board: (any or all of the following)

What would you do if you saw a UFO?

What would you do if a very small man (180 cm tall) approached you on the street, pointed a knife at you, and asked for all of your money?

If you could know the exact time and date of your death, would you want to?

If you could have any super power – for example, the ability to fly, or to be very strong, or to become invisible – which super power would you choose? Why? What would you do with this power?

If you could go back in time and kill Hitler, would you?

If someone offered you $10,000 to take naked pictures of you and put them on the internet, would you do it?

If you could save 100 monkeys by killing one person, would you do it?

If you could meet any three famous people, which three people would it be, and why?

If you could end world hunger by cutting off one of your arms, would you do it?

If you had a time machine and could travel to any three times in history, which three times would you want to visit, and why?

If you had $5,000 and you had to spend it within 24 hours, what would you do?

If you could kill people only by thinking about it, do you think you would use this power? Who would you kill and why?

Would you work for a company that you knew polluted the environment with toxic waste if they offered you a salary of $20,000 a month?

If you could live a very comfortable life in a country of your choice, but never return to your country or see your family or friends again, would you go?

If you could live to be 100 years old but stay young and healthy in appearance, would you want to? 200? 500?

If you could change three things about the world today, what would you change?

If you could change one thing about your body, what would it be?

What would you do if you knew that the world was going to be hit by a comet and destroyed in one week?

What would you do if your teacher came to class drunk?

What would you do if you woke up and there was a dead hooker's head in your toilet?

You: "Get in pairs, and ask these questions. And any other questions you can think of with 'What would you do if…'"

You can leave the last couple out if you happen to be coming to class drunk, or if you woke up and there really was a dead hooker's head in your toilet.

48) MORE FUN WITH PICTURES

LEVEL: All

This isn't so much an activity as a kind of activity; there are a million different things you can do with pictures.

Get a bunch of pictures from the internet – pictures from news stories are usually good, with a lot of different locations and activities happening. Often there are so many pictures in your course book (if you have one) that you can use that – have the students flip around to different pages and find pictures that interest them.

You can use these damn things for a practically unlimited number of classroom activities.

Hand out the pictures:

<u>You:</u>

"Talk about what you see in the picture. Describe everything you see."

"What's happening in the picture? What are the people doing?"

"Talk about who these people might be, and how they might be feeling. Why might they be there?"

"Talk about which of the pictures you prefer, and why."

"Talk about how the picture makes you feel." (No actually – that's hippie crap. Don't ask that.)

"Talk about what happened before this picture was taken."

"Talk about what you think is going to happen next in the picture."

"Describe the clothes the people are wearing in the picture."

"Look at the picture. (Wait one minute.) Okay, now turn the picture over (or close the book) so you can't see it. Try to remember everything that was in the picture. What was happening? Where were the people?"

49) DECISION-MAKING CONVERSATIONAL ACTIVITIES

LEVEL: All

Again, this is more a kind of activity, than an activity itself. It can be adapted to many topics and grammar points.

As an example – say our grammar point is the future tense, and the vocabulary set is places in a city.

You: "Tell me some things that are fun to do (in this bleak industrial city) on the weekend."

As usual, you can do this with the ball or board it.

Students: "Get drunk! Go for a walk! Go shopping! Get in fights!"

You can board some of their answers.

You: "What are some ways we can invite somebody to do something, in English?"

Students: "Why don't we...?" "We could..." "How about _____-ing?" "We should..."

You: "Outstanding. Work in groups of two (or three or four). Make a plan. A group of friends from England or America (three people, young adults, with X amount of dollars) are coming to (our bleak industrial city) for a three-day holiday. Make a specific plan as to what they're going to do at the following times."

Board:

Friday evening

Saturday afternoon

Saturday evening and night

Sunday afternoon

Sunday afternoon and night

You: "Think about: sightseeing, foods they will eat for breakfast, lunch, and dinner, how they will get around, shopping, nightlife, problems, money. Do it!"

(And after they finish, have each group describe their plans, with "going to.")

This could take anywhere from 10 minutes to an hour, depending on the class.

There's plenty of other fodder for decision-making activities you could use to practice different grammar points and vocabulary, but that's usually a productive one.

Another one is planning a vacation:

You: "Imagine you and your partner won a contest and are going on a one-month vacation in Europe with $50,000 to spend. Decide where you are going to go and what you are going to do."

Or

"Imagine that you and your partner have three days to spend $10,000. What things would you do? What are you going to buy?"

Or

"Imagine that you won a contest and can travel around the world for one year, visiting one city in each of 20 different countries. What cities are you going to see, and what are you going to do there?"

Or

"Imagine that you are having a dinner party and can invite any 10 famous people – alive now, or at any time FROM HISTORY. Which 10 famous people will you invite?"

Or

"Imagine that you are Kings of the World, for one day. What things would you change about the world?"

Or (for a business class)

"Imagine that you have $1,000,000 to invest in local companies. Which companies would you invest in and why?"

And then at the end of the class you can have the groups describe their decisions, and justify them, and give a big fat kiss to the students who have the best plan.

(**Helpful Hint:** I warn you – often, these kinds of activities don't produce nearly as much English as you might think. Often students will simply defer to one student in the group, especially an older or richer one, and not having any particular interest in these things, or not knowing much about the topic and not having much imagination, will just say fine, fine, in order to get the activity completed quickly – which is probably what they think you want them to do.)

50) AN ACTIVE PASSIVE ACTIVITY

LEVEL: Upper-Intermediate to Advanced

Some kinds of grammatical structures are easy to make up speaking activities about. Past tense? Talk about what you did last weekend. Future tense? Make a plan for an imaginary trip around the world. Present perfect? Say, have you ever seen a grown man naked?

Others, however, defy such simple yet effective ploys, and one of these is the passive.

The passive is formed by using "is" or "are" plus the third form of the verb. We use it when the object of the sentence is more interesting or important to us than what or who did something. For example:

A lot of pornography IS FILMED in Eastern Europe now.

Glock handguns ARE MADE in Austria.

Because, of course, the pornography is of much more interest to us than the Eastern Europeans who make it. In the second case it's obvious who makes Glock handguns –the Glock company – so we don't need to say who did it.

We can use the passive if we don't know who did something, also, and there's no problem with changing it to the past tense:

Holy shit! My passport WAS STOLEN while I was passed out drunk!

Now this is all very well and good, but what do you do after your students have diligently transformed a bunch of sentences in the text book from active to passive and back to active again? How can we make a speaking activity to get them to use it?

Well, try this.

Board: Draw something like this:

Where	are		made
			written
When	is	?	directed
			invented
―――	was		discovered
			built
Who	were		killed (by)
			painted

You: "By applying this formula, you can make different questions in the passive. Notice that you must replace the '?' with something relevant."

Demonstrate:

You: "Who was the movie TITANIC directed by?"

Hot Chick: "Leonardo DiCrappio."

You: "Ah, no. Anybody else?"

Dorky Student: "James Cameron?"

You: "Complete sentence."

Dorky Student: "TITANIC was directed by James Cameron."

You: "Right. Okay, when was TITANIC made?"

Hot Chick: "I think about the time my dad was born."

You: "Ah, shit, okay, when was AVATAR made?"

Hot Chick: "It was made in 2009!"

You: "Excellent. Now get into pairs and ask some questions."

Or you could have some kind of class contest.

Most of them won't know much of anything about anything, of course, and that can be a problem. Hopefully when the students make questions for each other, they will be more likely to make a question that the other student knows the answer to, but this won't always be the case, especially if you are teaching a class with greatly mixed ages.

For particularly dense or recalcitrant classes you might have to write out a list of facts, first, on the board or on photocopies:

Board:

Mark David Chapman killed John Lennon.

Gustave Eiffel designed the Statue of Liberty.

Van Gogh painted SUNFLOWERS.

Gregory Dark, the porn director, directed the Britney Spears "OOPS!...I DID IT AGAIN" video.

Then they can definitely make answers to the passive questions. In the passive, of course.

That takes a lot more time, but remember, once you've compiled your list, you can use it again and again.

And after they've asked each other some questions, play a game of "TEST THE TEACHER'S INCREDIBLY LARGE BRAIN." Have them ask you some passive questions and see how many you know the answer to.

Probably a bunch. You're way the fuck more knowledgeable than most of your students, believe it.

51) RANKING ACTIVITIES

LEVEL: All

In a very similar vein to the last activity, consider whipping out this one.

This one is called "Desert Island."

You could introduce the topic by asking about those survival reality TV shows on islands, if the students have seen them.

You: "What kinds of problems would you have if you were stuck on an island? Work with your partner – make a list of 10 problems you would have."

Dorky Student: "Is there a source of fresh water?"

You: "Yeah, one little stream."

Dorky Student: "And food?"

You: "Some banana trees. That's all. A few monkeys."

Hot Chick: "Ooh, cute."

Dorky Student: "Until they rip your face off, cute."

You: "Okay, here's the situation: You and your partner are taking part in a reality TV show about people trying to live on a desert island for one month. Think of 10 things you want to take with you – nothing can be larger than about 1.5 meters by 1.5 meters.

Make a list, and put them in order from most to least important. Be specific – don't just say 'a book!' Say the name and author of the book! And talk about why!"

Board:

We should take _____ because _____.

We might _____.

So then, afterwards, groups work together to compare lists. Have them explain why they chose the things they did, in the order they did.

There are various other activities you could use for a "ranking activity."

You:

"Think of the 10 most important people in history and put them in order."

"Think of the 10 most important things in your house."

"Think of 10 countries you would like to visit, and put them in order, explaining why."

"Think of 10 jobs you would never like to do, and put them in order and explain why."

"Think of 10 of the biggest problems facing young people in your country today." (Ooh, topical.)

"Think of 10 places to hide the body of a dead business rival."

"Think of 10 ways to study English at home."

"Think of the 10 most important inventions in history."

Or:

Board:

TV

telephone

computer

atomic energy

cars

planes

printing press

microwave oven

washing machine

You: "Talk about which of these things are most important to you, and put them in order from the most important, to the least important."

(**Helpful Hint:** Again, these activities probably won't produce more than a few minutes worth of English, unless you have a particularly enthusiastic class. It happens, I guess. Sporadically. Very sporadically.)

52) TOPICAL EXTENDED SPEAKING

LEVEL: Intermediate to Advanced

This is similar to dice games or the question challenge.

But, instead of back-and-forth questions, one student will try to speak for one (or two, or three, or five) minutes without stopping, while the partner listens for mistakes. You can just do it by choosing a topic.

You: "Tell me some usual conversation topics."

Students: "Cars! Sushi! Computer games! The mind-body problem!"

Board:

1) Cars

2) Sushi

3) Computer games

(Etc.)

You: "Now – the partners on the left will try to speak for one minute about the first topic of cars."

Dorky Student: "Ah, is that your left or...?"

You: "Students sitting on THIS SIDE (indicating) will try to speak for one minute about the first topic – cars. Okay, ready? Think of your question words – what kind, where, when, why, etc. Ready, go!"

(Take out a timer and turn it on, and let the little pumpkin-heads babble on for one minute.)

You: "Now, the partner on the right, try to speak about sushi for one minute."

Dorky Student: "It's difficult!"

Hot Chick: "Sushi, it's an easy topic."

You: "Of course it's difficult, that's why we're doing it. GO!"

(Again, take out your timer.)

You can do a few different topics for one minute, and depending on the students' reactions, move on to speaking for two minutes about the next topic. Then three minutes, etc., depending on how easy or difficult it is for the students.

Then you could have somebody volunteer to speak in front of the class, or just choose some little mook you don't like to do it as a punishment.

53) PERFECTING THE PAST PERFECT

LEVEL: Upper-Intermediate to Advanced

Here's another tense that's a real crotch to do in class: the past perfect.

You: "Class, what is the past perfect tense? What time do we talk about with it?"

Dorky Student: "The past perfect tense is formed by using had + the past participle – that's the third form of the verb. It indicates that something happened, and finished, BEFORE SOME OTHER ACTIVITY in the past."

Or not. More likely you'll have to explain it.

Board:

He looked down. His wallet was gone – the hooker HAD STOLEN it while his pants were down!

You: "When did the hooker steal his wallet? Before or after he looked down?"

Students: "Before!"

You: "But how do we know that? In this example, the verb comes AFTER 'he looked down.'"

Students: (triumphantly) "Because it's the past perfect tense, yo!"

Essentially a stupid tense, anyway. So you get the students to work through all the gap-filling exercises in the book and maybe write some example sentences -- then what? Fuck, how the hell do you talk about some shit that happened before something else in the past? You've got no reference there.

I struggled with it for ages. I managed to come up with a few examples of questions to ask:

"Had you ever met a foreigner before you saw me?"

"Had you smoked before you turned 16?"

And a few other pitiful examples.

Finally I realized there was no need to keep it real – I elaborated on some activities I saw elsewhere and came up with the following low-fuss but productive speaking activity.

Board:

Why was the girl crying?

Why were the streets empty?

Why was the man's nose bleeding?

Why was the house empty?

Why was the crowd cheering?

Why was the dog barking?

Why was her dress dirty?

Why was the car burning?

Why was the young couple smiling?

Why was the crowd angry?

Why was the TV gone?

I think you get the idea. Write as many sentences as you can, because students rarely want to say more than they have to.

You: "Speak to your partner. You have to think of a reason why there things happened, or were happening."

Demonstrate:

You: "Why was the man's nose bleeding? Because somebody had kicked his ass for no particular reason, or maybe because he was a foreigner. So, Dorky Student – why was the girl's dress dirty?"

Dorky Student: "Because the dirty slut queen had been rolling around in the mud!"

Hot Chick: "But why would she…?"

You: "It's immaterial – we're just trying to produce English in the past perfect here. Why was the crowd angry?"

Rich Guy: "Because their English teacher had told them to stop using mobile phones."

(**Helpful Hint:** EMPHASIZE THAT IT HAS TO BE SOMETHING THAT HAPPENED AND FINISHED BEFORE the action in question. Otherwise you'll get answers like:

Q: Why was the crowd angry?

A: Because wild dogs were chasing them through the streets.

Which isn't our target language. That's the past continuous.)

You might offer that as an example of what they're NOT supposed to do. Never underestimate the stupidity of your students. Or, hell, if you want to get fancy, and review the past continuous:

You: "Now make a past perfect AND a past continuous reason for each example. Something that finished before, and something that was in progress at that time."

They'll be licking your ass as a grammar god afterward.

PART THREE: FUN WITH YOUR PRIVATES

In which we discuss the pains and problems of attempting to teach a student one-on-one, and solve those problems with page after page of lists

THE PAIN OF PRIVATES

Now here's another part of English teaching that can be surprisingly painful.

Individual lessons.

Teaching one person, I mean.

All the problems you have making a group speak are even MORE true for an individual.

Assume that the student has absolutely nothing to say. You'll usually be correct.

"Private students," as a colleague once pointed out, would actually be defined as students that you are teaching on your own, outside of your normal work arrangement, for extra money, whereas students you're teaching one-on-one as part of your normal working arrangement might be more accurately called "individual students."

What-fucking-ever; I'll be using the two terms more or less interchangeably.

There are a lot of reasons teachers hate doing one-on-one lessons through their schools – not least because the student is probably paying three or four times what they'd pay for a normal class, but the teacher is getting paid exactly the same as he always does despite having to work a lot harder.

But mainly it gets down to the tedium factor. A small minority of individual students will have much of anything to say, and the rest will just smile uncomfortably at you while you desperately try to jump-start a conversation or run monotonously through the book with them, leaving out all the games and songs and other stuff that makes class halfway interesting.

We had loads of them in Bangkok in my first job; they gave our individual lessons away at bargain prices outside of the 10:00 am to 12:00 pm and 6:00 pm to 8:00 pm peak hours.

They were generally unhappy teenagers being forced to study by their parents, sitting with a terrified grin the whole time, and answering virtually every question with a nod of the head and a broad smile.

And in a one-on-one class, baby, there's NO WAY OUT. You can't take a break, most likely, and students will probably bitch to the management about too many songs or too much time spent reading. It's ALL YOU, stuck in a small room with somebody you've got nothing at all in common with on any level beyond the cellular.

I can remember them all quite clearly.

There was the middle-aged guy who worked at the TV station, whose wife had just died, who had never studied English and answered every question with a sober nod of the head and a "Hmmmm."

There was the little fat girl who always looked like she was about to cry, she was so frightened.

There was the little gay fashion designer named Aye with the punk hairdo who smiled and made cow eyes at me during the whole lesson. (The secretary loved to tell me – "Piwate student Aye like man, like X! Like man!" and then burst into hysterical giggles.)

Then there was the fat kid. He was pretty typical.

We had a lot of fat kids in Bangkok. Obviously they were rich kids, and in the grand Thai tradition were spoiled rotten and given each and every thing they wanted – and that usually included a lot of fast food. Our school was in a shopping mall – in the summer, students were dropped off in the morning, where they ate a big fast food breakfast; went to some classes at our school in the morning, after which they had a big fast food lunch; and then spent the afternoon shopping, at the cinema, at the water park, or at the videogame arcade – after which they had a big fast food dinner.

We had 'em all in our mall – McDonald's, KFC, Burger King, Pizza Hut. Even my personal favorite, Popeye's Cajun Fried Chicken.

The fat kid was about 13 or 14, but probably weighed close to 200 pounds. None of it was muscle. He had a bodyguard, a strange-looking guy with an Elvis haircut who sat by the entrance while the fat kid studied.

The fat kid had asthma. His breath rattled disgustingly in his lungs. He made weird wheezing noises constantly. He was a pack-a-day smoker already, and was being forced to study by his parents, as he would soon be shipped off to Australia to learn English the hard way.

I sat in a small enclosed room with him. The stench of McDonald's lard coming out of his pores was overpowering. I had him read the book and then asked him if he understood. "Understand," he would say. "So what's the difference between the present perfect and the past simple?" I'd ask. He'd nod his head. "Understand."

"So what did you do yesterday?" I'd ask.

"Watch TV." He'd smile in the incredibly uncomfortable way that a person living in Thailand quickly realized was a signal of abject desire to be someplace else.

"Watched TV. Past tense."

"Yes. Understand."

"What did you watch?"

A long pause. "No remember."

"What kind of TV programs do you like, in general?"

He'd smile and nod. "I like watch TV."

"Do you like movies?"

"Like."

"What kind of movies do you like?"

"Yes, like."

"Did you see BATMAN FOREVER?"

"Yes."

"What did you think of it?"

"Like."

"You should say, 'I liked it.' Past tense."

"Understand."

Long pause.

"What did you like?"

Pause.

"No remember."

This gay banter continued for 90 minutes or so. Three days a week.

(But don't let me give you the impression the fat kid was different from most Thais – that would be a fairly usual exchange between a teacher and a student. It's just the agony of being trapped alone in a room with a fat kid stinking of hydrogenated vegetable oil and salt that I'm trying to get across here.)

I remember one guy I taught in Russia.

To describe him as exhausted and uninterested would be a grand bit of understatement.

"What did you do this weekend?"

"Worked."

"And after work?"

"Uh…I watched TV."

"What did you watch?"

"I don't remember. I was too tired."

It seemed to me he didn't even need to speak ONE language, much less two.

So what can you do?

Well, those activities in Part Two can work well enough with a low-level individual.

Force them to make complete sentences, and force them to ask YOU questions. (See how they like it when you answer with monosyllabic grunts.)

A very unpleasant scenario that happens often:

Administration Crony: "English Teacher X, you have a new individual student tomorrow at 4:00 pm."

You, grumbling: "What level is she studying?"

Administration Crony: "She doesn't want to use a book. She just wants to talk."

You: "I assume she took a placement test, though. Let me guess – intermediate."

Administration Crony: "Correct."

The following chapter presents a plan of attack.

PAINKILLERS FOR PRIVATE LESSONS

Basically the following chapter contains lists of questions and detailed instructions for getting through the first three lessons; those are usually the hardest ones. And often the only ones, as the student realizes she's far too busy to study English.

Each lesson probably contains 45 minutes to an hour of material; it's quite possible, if you get a talkative student, or a student who constantly runs off to answer the phone or whatever, that the material could stretch out to cover two or even three lessons.

That's fine, of course. EXPLOIT THAT MATERIAL.

The lesson plans contain mostly lists of questions to cover the topic, but also include an optional grammar presentation and a worksheet, as students often somehow feel they're not studying English properly if they don't get stuff like that.

And we're professionals, right?

So print all this stuff out and take it to class with you, and it'll probably be enough.

It's better to take extra stuff though, generally – photocopy and print out some scary grammar activities you can threaten the student with if they don't want to speak.

FIRST GENERIC INTRODUCTORY LESSON FOR INDIVIDUALS
LEVEL: Intermediate to Advanced

LESSON FOCUS: Present Simple, Job Duties and Responsibilities, Using English

Greet the student and introduce yourself, and make whatever introductory small talk seems appropriate or necessary.

(These questions have a business focus – you could switch "work" to "study" for a younger learner.)

You: "Today's lesson is focused mainly on speaking using the present simple tense, and describing job duties and responsibilities. Hopefully, this will also show me your strengths and needs with grammar and speaking."

"Do you know what the present simple tense is? What time are we talking about with it?"

(Now obviously – sometimes – things will stop quite dead in their tracks right here, as the student doesn't understand a damn thing that you say. Go back to Part Two and start doing those activities, in this case.)

If the student shows some ability, keep moving forward, and explain that present simple talks about things we do habitually, or every day.

QUESTION PRACTICE – Work and Job Responsibilities

You might choose to begin with the optional grammar presentation (see below) if the student seems to be very weak with grammar. You'll know by the time you do the first four bulleted questions.

(Ask the student whichever of these questions is appropriate, feeling free to expand on them as necessary. REMEMBER TO STICK WITH THE PRESENT SIMPLE, unless the student is obviously very comfortable with switching tenses.)

You: "Answer these questions in the present simple tense."

What do you do? (Remind the student this means "What's your job?")

Where do you work?

What's your job title / position? (This can be discussed – brainstorm some different jobs in the field.)

What's the name of the company? Where is your office?

Are you married?

Do you have any brothers or sisters? Where does your (wife / sister / brother) work?

Does your mother or father work? What do they do?

What do you do in your job? What are your job responsibilities?

Here you can stop and brainstorm some things people do in their business jobs – a likely list:

write, read, send, receive, get, meet with, negotiate with, travel to, inspect, check, make, do, research, design, plan, work with

If the student seems to be confidently intermediate in ability, use attached worksheet #1 – if not, stick with the verbs above, or even omit some of the less common ones.

By this point you should have a pretty good idea whether the student can or will speak correctly; if he / she fucked up all those questions, teach a bit about present simple tense and then go back and do the questions again until the student can answer them correctly.

If the student rocked on the questions, ask more:

Why do you want to study English now?

How often do you study English?

What is difficult / easy about studying English for you?

What do you like / not like about studying English?

What problems do you think you have with speaking, listening, writing, and reading?

How often do you speak English in your job? How often do you speak English in person? How often do you speak English on the telephone?

How often do you read or write English in your job? What do you read? What do you write?

Who do you write to? Do they write (reports, emails) to you?

How often do you deal with or speak with colleagues from America or England? Who are these colleagues?

When do you meet them? What do you think of these colleagues? What are they like? What are their names? Where are they from? What do they do?

How often do you deal with or speak with colleagues from Europe? Where are these colleagues from? What are their native languages? Do they speak English well?

How often do you travel to other cities or countries in your job? Which countries do you travel to? Why? What do you do there?

If they travel abroad, ask:

Do you have problems speaking with people in hotels in English? Do you have problems speaking with people in restaurants in English? Do you have problems speaking with people in shops in English? Why do you have problems?

How often do colleagues from other countries visit you in (whatever industrial shithole you live in)? What problems do you have when you speak with them?

Where do these colleagues stay? What do they do when they come here? What do they do in their free time here? Do they like it / dislike it?

Who is your superior? Who do you report to? (Discuss these terms, and if the student is receptive, make a chart of the corporate structure on the board and discuss the job titles of the people the student works with.)

Who do you usually work with? What do you think of these people? What are they like?

(You might explain that "What is Bob like?" means "Tell me about Bob," and compare it with "What does he like doing?" or "What does he look like?" This point is complicated and the student might be glad if you explain it a bit.)

How often do you use the telephone in your job? What do you do on the telephone?

How often do you use a computer in your job? What do you do with your computer?

How often do you use the internet in your job? Do you ever read websites in English? Why? Which ones?

What time do you usually get to work? What time do you usually finish work?

How many hours do you work in a usual week? How many weeks of holiday do you have in a usual year?

What time do you usually have lunch / dinner? Where do you usually have lunch / dinner?

What foods do you like / dislike? Why? What are you favorite restaurants / cafés in (your city, a nearby city, a city the student visits often)?

Do you work on weekends? How often do you work weekends? How do you feel about this?

How often do you have a holiday / vacation? (Make sure the student knows the difference between "day off" and "holiday.")

What do you usually do in the evenings / in your free time / on your holidays / on your birthday / at Christmas?

Obviously, this will give you a lot of information about the student's needs, desires, and problems. Make some notes about it – so that when the student gets a new teacher in a few weeks because of schedule problems, you can give them to the new teacher.

Now you can encourage the student to ask you some questions about your job and your life.

Board:

Who

What

Where

Why

How often

How many

How much

You: "Now, try to ask me 20 questions about MY job."

(Or, of course, fewer questions if the student is really weak.)

This might well convince the student that studying "speaking without a book" is a really stupid fucking idea. That'll take the pressure off you.

When the student asks questions like "How long have you worked here?" don't spend too much time on it – stick with present simple, if possible, unless the student is obviously comfortable with tenses, then let the conversation flow wherever the student wishes.

If the student has been pretty hopeless in the questions and answers, go ahead and do some of your photocopied grammar exercises in class together.

OPTIONAL GRAMMAR PRESENTATION: Do it only if student seems confused about the form / meaning of this tense – students often like grammar, but not always.

Board:

1) I live in Shitsville.

2) I am a teacher.

3) I am from England.

4) I work for Crappy Language School in Shitsville.

5) My name is Octavius.

You: "How can we change these answers using 'he' or 'she'?"

Erase "I" and write "He / She" or "They" or "You" in the blanks and see if the student can change the verbs appropriately.

You:

"What's the difference between 'I' 'me' and 'my'?"

"What are the questions for these answers? What are those questions with 'He' and 'She'?"

Questions should be: "Where do you live?" "What do you do?" "Where are you from?" "Where do you work?" "What's your name?"

I certainly hope you fucking knew that.

Point out that "What do you do?" means "as a profession" – contrast it with "What are you doing now?" if the student seems confused about it.

Point out that this is more polite than "What's your job?" which sounds blunt and rude and allows people to answer "I'm a student / housewife / retired" rather than "I don't have a job." Have a laugh at the expense of the unemployed.

You: "Why do we use 'do' in questions one, two, and four, and 'am' and 'is' in three and five?"

(I certainly hope that you fucking know the answer to that, also – we use "do" or "does" to make questions with verbs, and "is" or "are" to make other questions.)

Board:

Where _____ your car?

What _____ you usually do in your free time?

_____ you have any brothers or sisters?

_____ you from Shitsville?

What time _____ you get up?

You: "What are the correct words to complete these questions?"

(If the student seems weak or confused, translate the question words – "Who / What / Where / When / Why / How often / How many / How much." If the student is strong, ask about the difference between "How much?" and "How many?"

Also optional, if student has trouble expressing times:

TIME:

Board:

What time is it?

Draw a clock on the board, and write some digital times, and get the student to practice saying times correctly. (You might spend more, or less, time on this, depending on the student's ability.)

MORE QUESTIONS:

If the student has done everything with ease, yet you still have some time left, do the following:

<u>**You:**</u>

"Here are some present simple questions about other parts of your life."

What part of (your city) do you live in? What's your favorite part of Shitsville?

How often do you go to the theater / opera / bars and nightclubs / restaurants?

Which restaurants, bars, nightclubs do you like in Shitsville? In (some other city)? When do you go? Who do you go with? Why do you like them?

<u>**You:**</u> "Now ask ME 10 questions about my free time."

(You'll probably have to refer the student to "What time / Where / Who _____ with?" etc.)

Then move on to the following:

<u>**You:**</u> "Here are some questions about sports. First, tell me some sports in English. How many sports in English do you know?"

What sports do you like doing? How often do you do them? Where do you do them? Who do you do them with? Why do you like them?

What sorts do you like watching on television? Why / why not?

Do you like football / basketball / tennis / hockey? Why / not?

What sportspeople do you like? What do you think of Anna Kournikova / Maria Shirapova / David Beckham / the Olympics?

What do you think of boxing / water sports / winter sports / "extreme" sports like skydiving? Would you like to do any of these sports?

(You might want to point out the difference between "would like" and "like" – ask what the difference is between "I'd like to swim" and "I like swimming." (Answer: "I'd like" means "I want.")

You: "Okay, now try to ask ME 10 questions about sports."

If somehow time STILL hasn't run out, go ahead and do the following:

You:

"Here are some questions about movies, books, and TV shows. What are some different kinds of movies? Books? TV shows?"

(You could board these things; it looks professional and kills some time.)

What kinds of movies / books / TV shows do you like?

How often do you watch TV / read / go to the cinema?

What actors / actresses do you like, and why?

What kind of movies / books / TV shows do you NOT like?

What do you think of (reality shows, violent horror movies, news programs, Michael Jackson, Miley Cyrus, Tom Cruise, etc.)?

If the student has breezed through all of this, consider talking about the office they work in: where different things or people are there.

Where's the fax machine / the toilet / the computer / the boss's office / the water cooler (etc.)?

Talk about their flat: what's in it, where it is, and what's in the different rooms.

Talk about locations in the city: where the shopping centers are, good areas, bad areas, famous places, etc.

On the next page is a worksheet you can use:

WORKSHEET ABOUT JOB RESPONSIBILITIES AND WORK

Match the verbs from the first group with the nouns in the second. Many combinations are possible! Consider them all!

Group A: Verbs

Write   Purchase   Read   Speak with   Call   Use   Get   Send   Receive   Find   Look for   Research   Meet with   Check   Sell   Negotiate with   Take   Buy   Travel to   Arrange   Deal with   Make   Design   Plan   Deliver   Start   Finish   Solve   Use

Group B: Nouns

Clients   Reports   Faxes   Orders   Customers   Suppliers   Emails   Invoices   Bills   Documents   Contracts   Distributors   Colleagues   A meeting   A Business trip   Plans   An agreement   A deal   A project   Business letters   Phone calls   Deliveries   A package   Materials   Problems   Units   Containers   Equipment   the Internet   Computer tools   A conference   A seminar   A city / country   An office   A factory

Speaking Activity:

Which of these things do you do in your job? Which things do your colleagues do? Which of these do you enjoy / not enjoy? Why?

GENERIC SECOND LESSON PLAN FOR INDIVIDUAL STUDENTS
LEVEL: Upper-Intermediate to Advanced

LESSON FOCUS: Past Tenses (and a bit of Present Perfect) / Past Experiences and Holidays, Review of Job Routines and Responsibilities

WARMER / INTRO: Ask the student if he or she has any questions about homework or anything else, check homework, ask about any problems, etc. Then review some present tense stuff about jobs from last week:

What's your job, what do you usually do in your job, how often do you meet with your supervisor, etc.

MATERIAL: These questions. And maybe some photocopied grammar exercises about the past tense.

State that this lesson will focus on the past tense. Ask briefly if student knows the form of past tense questions and answers, and if they know the irregular forms of verbs. If there are problems, you might begin with some photocopied grammar exercises, or a list of irregular verbs.

PART I: WORK

You:

"Here are some past tense questions that focus on your job:"

When did you start working for this company?

What position did you have when you started? What responsibilities did you have in that position? Did you enjoy that position?

Who did you work with when you first started? What did you think of those people?

When did you start work yesterday and what did you do after you arrived?

How many telephone calls did you make yesterday? Who did you call? What did you discuss?

Did you use the internet yesterday? Why?

Did you write anything yesterday? What did you write? When did you have lunch yesterday? What did you do after lunch?

What did you do last week at work? What projects did you work on? What clients did you deal with?

Did you drive or travel anywhere for work?

Did you meet with any colleagues?

Did you speak English to anyone at your job?

What did you do last year at your job? What was the most interesting / important project that you worked on?

How many times did you speak English for work last year? Did you meet any colleagues from English-speaking countries?

What were the best / worst things that happened to you last year at work? (Be sensitive, of course – if there was an office shooting or something, omit this question.)

You: "Now ask me at least 10 questions about MY work in the past tense."

Board:

What time / where / when / why / who did

PART II: EDUCATION

You: "Here are some past tense questions that focus on education."

When did you finish university? What did you study?

What did you think of your teachers / your course / your faculty / your fellow students?

What were the best and worst things about your university education? What were your favorite / least favorite subjects?

What did you do in your free time when you were at university? (Perhaps you'll get lucky here and get some graphic tales of drugs and sex parties.)

What school did you go to? Where?

What subjects at your school did you like / not like? Who were your favorite / least favorite teachers? Why? What were the best and worst things about your school?

You: "Now make some questions about MY school and university, in the past tense."

PART III: TRAVEL

Most people who study English these days have traveled abroad – if your student hasn't, by some bizarre quirk, ask about trips within the student's home country, and omit questions about speaking English. Unless of course the student lives somewhere touristy, like Prague, where it's easier to get around in English than it is in Czech.)

When was the first time you traveled abroad? Where did you go? Where did you stay? What was the hotel / apartment like?

Why did you go there? What did you do there? What did you see there?

Where did you have breakfast / lunch / dinner? What did you think of the food?

What did you do in the evenings? Did you go to any nightclubs or bars? What were they like?

Did you speak English there? What problems did you have speaking and understanding English? Did you meet any foreigners? What were they like?

(Helpful Hint: Again, you might need to point out the difference between the questions "What is he like?" and "What does he like?" here – explain that "What is something like?" means "Tell me about it.")

Which countries (or cities in your country) have you visited?

When was the second / third / fourth / most recent time you traveled abroad? (Then use the same follow-up questions above.)

What countries did you like the most / least? Why?

What hotels did you like the most / least? Why?

What sites / tourist attraction did you like the most / least? Why?

Where did you think the people where nicest, and why?

Do you ever travel for business? When was the first time / last time you traveled for business?

Where did you go? Why did you go there? What did you do there? Were there any problems with your work there? How did you get there? How was the journey? Who did you go with? When did you come back?

<u>You:</u> "Now ask ME at least 10 questions about traveling."

(Helpful Hint: Here there is a likelihood that the student will confuse present perfect and past simple / continuous at times – and likely the student will be so sick of your inquisition, that she will gladly roll with some grammar for a while. A grammar presentation is included below.

If the student is having trouble using past tense verbs correctly, ask her if she would like to review them, and go through the common expressions on the worksheet.)

PART IV: FREE TIME

What did you do last weekend? What did you do last Friday evening? (Where / when / why / what time / who with?)

What time did you get up on Saturday? What did you do during the day on Saturday? (Where / when / who with / why / what time / how?)

What did you do Saturday evening and night? (Who / what / where / when / etc.)

What time did you get up on Sunday? What did you have for breakfast / lunch / dinner? What did you do Sunday afternoon?

What did you do on your last birthday / last Christmas / last summer / on your mother's last birthday / last New Year's Eve / on Dec 31st, 1999?

(Now, of course, you should use local holidays, if you're teaching in China or the Middle East, not these.)

What did you like doing in your free time when you were a child? Where / when / how / who with?

When you were a teenager, what did you do in your free time? Where / when / how / who with?

After the student has satisfactorily answered most of these questions:

You: "Now ask ME at least 10 questions about yesterday and last weekend."

OPTIONAL GRAMMAR PRESENTATION: PAST SIMPLE VS. PAST CONTINUOUS

You can use whatever internet / resource book photocopied stuff about past simple vs. past continuous, etc., but don't bother too much with contrasting present perfect. Insist that you'll study that later.

Board:

I ate dinner at 8:00 pm yesterday.

I was eating dinner at 8:00 pm yesterday.

You: "What's the difference between these two questions?"

. . .

"In the first case, the dinner began at 8; in the second case it began before 8 and finished sometime after 8."

"Usually past simple indicates something that happened and finished; past continuous indicates that something was incomplete at some time in the past."

You: "Okay, now we're going to practice the difference between these two tenses."

Where were you at (different times) yesterday? What were you doing? (Emphasize that we are talking about unfinished actions in progress at this time.)

What time did you…yesterday? (We are talking about events that happened and finished.)

WORKSHEET: HOLIDAY VOCABULARY COLLOCATIONS

Match the verbs with as many different nouns as possible:

VERBS:

Go / Book / Rent (Hire) / Drive / See / Have / Go to / Go on

NOUNS:

To Paris   Abroad   A car

A holiday   A package tour   An excursion

A plane ticket   For a walk   To a museum

A nice holiday   A good trip   A restaurant

Swimming   A hotel room

A nice breakfast   A sea cruise   A bad flight

A famous statue   The sites   The scenery

Sightseeing

THIRD GENERIC LESSON PLAN FOR INDIVIDUALS
LEVEL: Upper-Intermediate to Advanced

LESSON FOCUS: Future Tense – Language for Meetings and Travel Plans, Arrangements and Dates, Review of Job Vocabulary

MATERIALS: "Rock Star Schedules," photocopied or printed grammar activities about going to and will.

You: "Today's lesson is going to be about using the future tense, and discussing meetings, plans, travel arrangements, and dates."

"So – what's the difference between 'going to' and 'will'"?

(You can kind of gloss over this if the student doesn't care, or if you don't feel like explaining the difference.)

Basically the answer is that:

"Going to" is to discuss our PLANS for the future. ("I'm going to vomit.")

"Will" is to discuss our NEW IDEAS, PREDICTIONS, or PROMISES about the future ("I'll call you, baby." "The world will end in 2012!") and SENTENCES WITH IF. ("If you fuck that fat chick, you'll regret it.")

You: "So, with that in mind, what's the difference between 'I'm going to watch TV' and 'I'll watch TV'?"

(The answer is basically that "I'm going to watch TV" is a plan, made before speaking, and "I'll watch TV" is a new idea, like "Hmmm, bad hangover, no money – I guess I'll watch TV tonight.")

You could do the grammar presentation first, or do the example questions first.

PART I: GOING TO

What time are you going to finish work today?

What are you going to do after work?

What time are you going to go home?

What are you going to have for dinner? What are you going to do after you have dinner?

Are you going to watch TV tonight? What are you going to watch?

What time are you going to go to bed?

(This might be a good time to mention that "might" is a perfectly acceptable way to talk about the future – "I might go home and watch TV but I might go shopping." In addition, "I'd like to" is often used – point out that it basically means the same thing as "I want.")

What time are you going to go to work tomorrow?

What are you going to do at work tomorrow?

What time are you going to have lunch?

Are you going to speak English at work tomorrow?

Are you going to write anything? Are you going to use the internet?

Are you going to write or read anything in English this week at work?

Are you going to travel for business anytime soon?

When's the next time you're going to study English? How much time are you going to spend (studying English, etc.) this week?

What are you plans for next weekend?

(Encourage the student to use "might" if she doesn't know, or that the answer "I don't have any plans yet" is an acceptable answer.)

When are you going to have your next holiday? (Emphasize the difference between "holiday" and "vacation" and "weekend.") *Where are you going to go? Who are you going to go with?*

What are your plans for Christmas / your next birthday / the next public holiday / the summer / the winter?

(If the student has children, you can ask what the plans for the children's future are – this might be better used with "I hope she / he will" if the child is young, however – refer to next section.)

NOTE: Often students are surprisingly reluctant about telling you their plans for the future, mainly because they don't have any. If you are finding this to be the case, and the student is constantly answering "I don't know" then you could just tell them to make something up.

You: "Remember, the point here is to speak English, not to give me correct information." (Checkmate!)

(You could also switch to using "would like" in the questions – "What would you like to do next weekend? Where would you like to go? Who would you like to go with? Which countries would you like to visit?")

You: "Now ask ME 10 questions with 'going to.'"

(And just make up all your answers. "I'm going to fly to Mars tonight on my Pegasus!" The student will think it's fucking hysterical. Or that you're retarded. Or on drugs. Or both.)

PART II: WILL

You: "We're going to practice 'will.' Remember, how do we use 'will'?"

(Never tell when you can ask, of course.)

"That's right, for new ideas and predictions about the future rather than plans.

You can answer these questions many ways."

Board:

I hope so.

I hope not.

I think so.

I don't think so.

(But of course, you'll also ask WHY?)

You:

Do you think that the economy of your country will improve this year, or get worse?

Do you think that the price of oil will go up again, or down?

Who do you think will be the next President of your country / the next mayor of your city / the next President of the United States?

(Most students have little interest in politics and global affairs, in my experience, but who knows, one might surprise you.)

Do you think that your company will do good business in your city / your country / internationally this year? Why?

Do you think that you will ever change your job? When? Why? What would you like to do?

Do you think there will be any major changes in your work or your responsibilities this year or next year?

Do you think the weather will be cold this summer? Why?

Do you think the United States or (your country) will ever have a female president?

Do you think that there will ever be a war between China and Russia / China and America / Russia and Europe and America?

(Naturally, this might be an insensitive question, if the country happens already to have had a war. I assume you wouldn't be teaching in a country where a war is actively being waged, but stranger things have happened.)

Do you think people will ever live in space? Do you think people will ever visit Mars?

Do you think there will ever be a cure for cancer / the common cold / AIDS? Why / why not?

(In my experience, students aren't going to have much to say on any of these topics, as they require both imagination and knowledge of current events, which few students will have.

Nonetheless the point will be made. This is fucking speaking.)

I'd suggest that the student will burn through these questions quickly in a blur of "I don't know" and "I have no plans" so you might move to this cunty grammar point, that might otherwise well be avoided.

PART III: PRESENT CONTINUOUS FOR FUTURE ARRANGEMENTS

Are you going to have any business meetings this week? With who? When? Where? What time? What are you going to talk about at these meetings?

Board:

I'm going to meet my mother tonight at 5:00 pm.

I'm meeting my mother tonight at 5:00 pm.

You: "What's the difference between these two statements?"

. . .

"We often use present continuous, with a future time reference, to discuss DEFINITE, PLANNED ARRANGEMENTS BETWEEN PEOPLE, or BETWEEN PEOPLE AND COMPANIES. But in such cases, we can use 'going to' also. But NOT 'will.'"

The included worksheets – Rock Star Schedule A and Rock Star Schedule B – are two diaries full of activities for the next week. I DON'T HAVE ANY PLANS is no longer an option. This is one time a photocopying role-playing type thing is NECESSARY.

Give the student Rock Star Schedule A and ask some questions in the present continuous.

Obviously you would want to use famous people that your students have heard of. Although, when it comes right down to it, it's not absolutely necessary – it just makes the game a bit less interesting if they don't know the people.

And it's not THAT interesting even if they recognize the names of famous people.

You:

"What are you doing on Monday morning?"

"Who are you having dinner with on Wednesday?"

"Who are you meeting on Tuesday night?"

"Where are you going on Wednesday?"

(Etc.)

"Now ask ME some questions about MY schedule."

ROCK STAR SCHEDULE A:

<u>MONDAY:</u>

Breakfast with Madonna (10:00 am)

Dinner with Robert De Niro (9:00 pm)

<u>TUESDAY:</u>

Tennis with Kanye West (2:00 pm)

Nightclub with Johnny Depp (10:30 pm)

<u>WEDNESDAY:</u>

Breakfast with Prince William (9:00 am)

Lunch with Barack Obama (12:00 pm)

Flying to New York (10:45 pm)

<u>THURSDAY:</u>

Lunch with Spielberg (2:00 pm)

Sailing with Lady Gaga (4:00 pm)

<u>FRIDAY:</u>

Breakfast with George Bush Jr. (10:00 am)

Sauna with Rhianna (3:30 pm)

<u>SATURDAY:</u>

Lunch with Jackie Chan (1:00 pm)

Swimming with Britney Spears (3:00 pm)

Dinner with Hosni Mubarak (8:00 pm)

<u>SUNDAY:</u>

Flying to Japan (10:00 am)

ROCK STAR SCHEDULE B:

<u>MONDAY:</u>

Flying to London (8:30 am)

Nightclub with Lady Gaga (11:00 pm)

<u>TUESDAY:</u>

Breakfast with James Cameron (9:00 am)

Driving to Switzerland (3:00 pm)

<u>WEDNESDAY:</u>

Skiing with David Beckham (10:00 am)

Casino with Brad Pitt (7:00 pm)

<u>THURSDAY:</u>

Flying to Hong Kong (9:00 am – 9:00 pm)

<u>FRIDAY:</u>

Lunch with Megan Fox (2:00 pm)

Dinner with Bill Gates (8:00 pm)

<u>SATURDAY:</u>

Tennis with Hillary Clinton (10:00 am)

Dinner with Bruce Willis (8:00 pm)

<u>SUNDAY:</u>

Breakfast with Justin Bieber (9:30 am)

Lunch with Angeline Jolie (2:00 pm)

Dinner with Nicholas Cage (9:00 pm)

FINAL COMMENTS ABOUT PRIVATE LESSONS

After this onslaught, if the student doesn't stop studying entirely, you could begin doing topic questions. (See Part Four.)

The best way to approach this is under the guise of the "needs analysis":

You: "Okay, now we've covered the main grammar points and the basic topics about you and your work. Can you tell me some topics that you want to talk about for your future lessons, since you don't want to use a book?"

(Of course the student by this point will probably be exhausted with your questions, and will happily decide to study in a course book with plenty of relaxing reading activities and songs for you to enjoy.)

If NOT:

Have the student write down 10 topics that they are interested in; you will, after reading Part Four, begin writing lists of questions related to the topic. Or just get those bastards off the internet.

Your final weapon: ask the student to write down a list of questions to ask *you*, about various topics that you choose.

That will surely get her back to studying the book.

PART FOUR: TOPIC-BASED SPEAKING QUESTIONS

In which we deal with classes full of eager beavers, of abundant abilities but limited knowledge of the world, and again find that lists are the answers to most of our problems

SPEAKING AT THE HIGHER LEVELS

So at the upper-intermediate and advanced levels, the students will be able to speak.

And even better, they'll be able to understand you when you talk to them.

This eases things along immensely.

But just because they CAN speak doesn't mean they WILL speak.

You still have to drag the students kicking and screaming towards the language you want them to produce.

You can and should still use the "short speaking activities" from Part Two to practice and review grammar points. You'll have to be a fairly competent ringmaster here, and move quickly from activity to activity so the students won't get bored, but you can still use them effectively.

But generally lessons will be based more on topics at this level, rather than on grammar points. At the upper-intermediate and advanced levels, your best move is to write a bunch of questions down and give them to the students; they assumedly have a good grasp of vocabulary and grammar and all at this point, and they should be trying to mix them up freely.

HOW TO USE THESE IN CLASS

Running an advanced conversation class probably isn't the most difficult thing you're going to do. Remember the old rule of three, and remember to review your vocabulary.

Now, the problem here is HOW MANY questions you need. If you're trying to run a conversation class without books, you need a LOT. If you're just using these questions to flesh out the course book, you don't need nearly as many.

Suppose you're running a conversation class with no text book:

Imagine the topic is computers.

You'd probably follow these steps:

1) Roll in and review computer vocabulary in one of the ways discussed earlier – lists, balls, worksheets, whatever. That might lead to some discussion right there.

2) Then you'd hand out a list of questions about computers, and have the students discuss them with their partners. Let that go on for as long as you wish.

(Now of course, you could also just write, for example, 10 questions on the board, and say, discuss the questions, and when the students are finished with them, write the next 10.)

3) Then, ask questions to the class, and see what they've got to say. Perhaps a lively classroom discussion will occur. Or perhaps you'll talk with a couple of students while the rest send text messages.

4) If you need to kill more time, you could also find some kind of text on the internet about computers and print it out and then do a reading activity before or after the questions; make sure you do some speaking activities after the reading, as detailed in the first part.

5) Need a listening activity? Take your laptop in, after carefully choosing and downloading some interesting crap about computers from YouTube.

6) Need a writing activity, or homework? Have the student write a composition of 300 (500? 1000?) words on the following topic: There are many ways to learn English by using the internet. (Or whatever. Scan the questions and find a likely topic.)

Voila. One lesson complete, baby.

EVEN MORE CHALLENGES FOR PERSONAL GROWTH AND SELF-DEVELOPMENT

Imagine that you have to teach a conversation class with the topic of education.

CHALLENGE ONE:

Think of about 20 questions on the topic of education, suitable for INTERMEDIATE level students.

CHALLENGE TWO:

Then think of 20 questions on the topic of education suitable for ADVANCED level students.

Okay, I'll wait.

Couldn't do it?

I understand. I was once weak and pathetic like you.

EXTENSIVE EXAMPLE OF SPEAKING QUESTIONS

Here's an example of a list of questions about education at the INTERMEDIATE level:

Now, notice they are in the present tense – this would be suitable if you're teaching university students or whatever. If you are teaching businesspeople, you'd have to change these to the past tense. Duh.

EXAMPLE DISCUSSION QUESTIONS – EDUCATION (INTERMEDIATE)

(These could be written on the board or on photocopied sheets.)

What is your favorite subject?

What subjects are you best at?

What subjects are you worst at?

What foreign languages do you learn?

Who is your favorite teacher? Why?

What is the most difficult subject?

What is the easiest subject?

How many days a week do you go to school?

How much homework do you have to do?

How do you get to school?

Do you want to go to university? Which university do you want to go to?

What do you want to be when you grow up?

What time do you start school? What time do you finish school?

Do you have school dinners? What are they like?

Who is your best friend at school?

How often do you have exams?

What is your happiest school memory? What is your worst school memory?

What do you usually have for lunch at school? Do you like it?

What job do you want in the future?

What teachers do you like and not like?

Now for comparison's sake, here's a list of questions at the ADVANCED level.

EXAMPLE DISCUSSION QUESTIONS – EDUCATION (ADVANCED)

Where did you go to school? What did you think of it? What subjects were you best and worst in? What did you like and dislike about your school? About your teachers? Who was your favorite teacher? What was your favorite subject?

Did you study English in school? What were your English lessons like? What did you like and not like about them?

Are most schools co-educational in your country – that is, mixed gender? What are the advantages and disadvantages of studying in single-sex schools? Would you like your children to study in single-sex schools? Why or why not?

Where did you go to university? What did you think of it? What subjects were you best and worst in? What did you like and dislike about your university? About your classmates? About your teachers? What were your favorite subjects? Who were your favorite teachers?

Did you study English at university? Where were your lessons like? What were your teachers like? What did you like and not like about them?

What was your major at university? Why did you choose this subject? Do you feel you received a good education in this subject? Why or why not?

Are there any subjects / classes you wanted to study but weren't available at your school / college? Were you allowed to choose some of the courses you wanted to study, or not? Do you think students should have a lot of choice in what subjects they study?

Do most students pay for their school educations in your country? Are private schools (that is, schools which must be paid for) better than public schools (that is, schools subsidized by the government)? Why or why not? Which do you think are better? Which do you / would you want your children to attend?

Are college tuitions reasonable in your country? Do you think university education should be paid for by the government? Are there any grant and scholarship programs available for students? Who gets these, and why?

What are the best / worst universities in (your city)? In your country? Why do they have reputations as being good / bad? What subjects do they specialize in?

What are the biggest problems with the educational system in your country? How could these problems be solved? Do you think the educational system is getting better, or worse? Why?

How much homework did you have to do as a child? At university? Do you think this was too much, or not enough? How much homework do you think children should be given?

Do you know anyone who is a teacher at a school or university? Do they like their job? Why or why not? What do they think of their salary? Do they want to change their job? Do they do anything to earn extra money?

Is it difficult for people without a college education to get good jobs in (your city)? In your country? Why or why not? What kinds of degrees are most / least useful?

What are some important factors in determining which college to attend? What are the qualities of a good student? What are the qualities of a good teacher?

Is it necessary to study English to get a good job in your city these days? Why or why not? What other skills are necessary to get a good job?

Should parents decide which university and which course of study their children should attend, or should the children make the decision themselves?

Should all students be made to study English, or should they be given a choice?

Why do you think people become teachers? What are the good and bad parts of being a teacher?

Do you think universities in other countries are superior to your country's universities? Would you consider studying abroad, or having your children study abroad? Why or why not? What course? What universities?

Have you ever heard of "home-schooling?" What do you think of home-schooling? Do you know anyone who was home-schooled?

Does a good education guarantee a good job? Why or why not? Does a good education guarantee success? Why or why not? Can you think of any examples of uneducated people who became very successful?

Which is more important, the essential skills in life you've learned to develop on your own, or the theoretical skills taught you in college? Do you think there should be a practical element to all education, or is theory enough?

When you were studying in school, what kinds of sports and social activities did you take part in? What did you think of them? Why did you choose these activities?

When you were studying at university, what kinds of sports and social activities did you take part in? What did you think of them? Why did you choose these activities?

Why do students often cheat during tests and exams? How do they cheat? Did you ever cheat on exams? Did your classmates? How did they cheat? What is your attitude towards this? Do you think this helps or harms the educational system in your country? What should teachers / universities do about cheating?

Do you think the education is a life-long process? What do you do now to continue increasing your knowledge?

Do you believe that "experience is the best teacher?" Why or why not?

Where do we learn most of the skills that help us later in life – in high school, or in college?

Are there any other skills that you think should be taught at school or university – for example, self-defense or cooking?

Do you think that sports (or physical education) should be a mandatory part of a school student's studies? A university student's? Why or why not? What are the advantages and disadvantages of mandatory physical education?

Do you think that religious studies should be a mandatory part of a university education? Why or why not? Political studies? Sex education? Drug and alcohol education?

Obviously I could provide you with dozens of pages of similar questions, or you could just find a lot of them on the internet, but I hope you get the idea and you can make your own list of questions, and hopefully questions which are suited to your particular students.

And of course, if you're teaching in Saudi Arabia or Yemen or whatever, you wouldn't want to ask the questions about mandatory drug and alcohol education or sex education.

PERSONAL GROWTH AND BETTERMENT CHALLENGE THREE:

Imagine the topic is computers.

1) Make a list of 50 questions related to computers, at the upper-intermediate or advanced level.

What, finished already?

Fine. Finally, the light of knowledge is breaking through your thick skull.

Here are several pages of examples.

SEVERAL PAGES OF EXAMPLES OF QUESTIONS ABOUT COMPUTERS

EXAMPLE DISCUSSION QUESTIONS – COMPUTERS (INTERMEDIATE)

Do you have a computer? What kind of computer do you have? What programs are installed on it? How much memory does it have?

How often do you use your computer? What do you usually use it for?

What are you favorite internet sites? How often do you visit them?

Can your mother and father use a computer?

Do you have a computer at work and at home?

Do you have a laptop or a desktop computer? Do you have both?

Do you use your computer when you do homework for school?

Have you ever studied English using your computer?

What kind of computer do you have?

What size is your computer screen? What size screen do you prefer?

What do you think is the best size to have?

Where do you use your computer?

Where in your room is your computer?

Why did you buy your computer?

Do you have a digital camera?

Do you send photos by email?

What kinds of pictures do you take with your digital camera?

Do you have a scanner? What kind of scanner do you have?

Do you have a blog, or use social network sites like FACEBOOK? Why? How often do you visit these sites?

Do you know any computer programming languages? How many computer programming languages do you know?

Do you read computer magazines? Which computer magazines do you read?

Did you learn to use a computer in high school?

Do you know how to type well?

How often do you use your computer?

What are some of your favorite computer games?

What do you use a computer for?

What operating system do you use?

What software do you use the most often?

When did you first start using a computer?

Who taught you to use a computer?

Do you use chat rooms? If so, what chat rooms do you use and who do you talk to?

Do you use email every day? Do you write emails in English? Have you ever sent an email to your teacher?

How many emails do you get a day? How many emails do you send a day?

Do you want a more powerful computer? If so, what computer do you want?

Have you ever taken a course at school where you used a computer?

How do you study English with your computer?

How does email work?

How many people in your family can use a computer?

How much did your first computer cost? How much did your last computer cost?

How much does it cost to buy a computer? What's the least expensive? What's the most expensive?

How much does your internet service provider cost? Which ISP do you use? Why?

What is the difference between software and hardware?

Which do you like better, a laptop computer or a desktop computer?

What is your favorite website?

Do you ever visit English websites?

Do you think our lives have been improved by computer technology? Could we live now without computers?

When did you first get a computer? What kind of computer was it? About how much did it cost? Do you still have it? Do you still use it?

Do you remember the first time you used a computer or the internet? What did you think about it?

How long have there been personal computers in your country? When did the average person start using a computer?

Can your parents operate a computer? Can your children use a computer?

How often do you perform a backup? What kind of backup method do you use? What kind of backup media do you use?

What are some good and bad things about having a computer?

Does having a computer make life more complicated or less complicated?

What computer games have you played? Which are your favorites? Which do you think are not so interesting?

What are chat rooms and instant messaging? Why can these be dangerous for you and your kids?

EXAMPLE DISCUSSION QUESTIONS – COMPUTERS (ADVANCED)

About how many hours a day do you use the internet? About how many hours a week do you use the internet?

When did you first use the internet? What did you look at?

Who uses the internet the most in your family?

What computer do you use to access the internet? Do you have a wireless or a dial-up connection?

Do you think computers are dangerous for our health? Why or why not?

Have you ever bought something using the internet? What did you buy? Why? What security issues do you have to think about when buying something through the internet?

Do you think that in the future, all shopping will be done on the internet? What items will / won't be bought on the internet? Why do you think so?

Do you think our lives have been improved by the internet? Why / not?

Do you think more men than women use the internet? What do they use it for?

What are some of the ways the internet can be used for education? Do you think that in the future all people might be taught over the internet?

What are some of the ways the internet can be used for entertainment?

What are the sites you most commonly access?

What problems does the internet create? What problems does it solve?

Which company is your internet provider? Why did you choose this company? Are you satisfied with their service? How much does it cost you?

Is it expensive to access the internet by mobile phone in your country? Do you ever access the internet from your mobile phone?

What types of pages do you access with your phone?

How much email do you receive and write in one day? Who do you write to and get email from? Why? Do you get a lot of "spam" email?

Why do you need more than one email address?

Have you ever chatted on the internet? Have you ever used an internet dating sight? What are the advantages and disadvantages of meeting people on the internet?

Some countries, like China and Saudi Arabia, control the content of internet websites people in the country can access. Do you think governments have the right to censor the internet? What are the advantages and disadvantages of this?

Do you think that the internet safe for children? Why or why not? Do you / Would you allow your children unmonitored access to the internet?

Do you think that it is important for schools to have internet access? Why?

Internet user-edited encyclopedias like Wikipedia are popular now – what do you think of these sites? What are the advantages and disadvantages of this?

Do you keep photos on the internet? Why or why not? What are the advantages and disadvantages of this?

Do you think that someday all books and magazines will be published on the internet? What are the advantages and disadvantages of this?

Do you think that it is a good or bad habit for young people to play computer games?

The internet can help people work from home. Do you think that this is good or bad? Could you do your job from home? Why or why not? What are the advantages and disadvantages of this?

Many disreputable companies get personal information from your computer when you visit their website. Why is this bad? What are the dangers of this? Are there any advantages to this?

Many people download MP3 music without paying any money for it. Do you think that this is a problem? Many people also download movies from the internet without paying for it. Do the authorities do anything to stop this in your country? What do they do? What do you think about this?

In your opinion, what is the most important feature of the internet?

Do you think that meeting people on the internet is easier than meeting people face to face?

Do you think that the internet will replace libraries?

Do you think that online banking (being able to do most of your banking by the internet and ATM machines) will become popular in all countries? What are the advantages and disadvantages of this?

In many big cities it is possible to buy your groceries online and have them delivered to your home. Why has this become popular?

What is a computer virus and how do we protect our computers from being infected?

How does the internet help people from different countries to communicate with each other?

How do we stop young children from looking at internet sites that have inappropriate content?

Do you think that some people spend too much time on the internet and does this stop them from seeing their friends? Why? Do you think that internet usage is an anti-social activity?

Do you think that having internet access is mainly for rich people? Will poor people be disadvantaged?

In some countries you can sell personal items on the internet (eBay). Do you think this is a good idea? Have you ever used eBay? For what?

Many universities are now offering online courses. What are the advantages and disadvantages of this?

Some websites hold very dangerous information; for example, how to make a bomb. How can we control these websites? Should there be complete freedom of information on the internet? Why or why not?

Which search engines do you use when you want to find information?

Search engines are used to find information. Do you think that they always give you the best sites or do they give you sites that pay money in order to be on the top of the list?

Many students use the internet to help them do their assignments or they just download complete reports or tests. How do we stop this? Did you do this when you were at university? What are the advantages and disadvantages of this?

We can use the internet to find jobs. What are the advantages and disadvantages of this for employers and employees?

Is the internet making people more impatient? Are we becoming a society where we all want instant satisfaction?

What restrictions should there be on using the internet at work?

A FINAL BATCH OF PERSONAL GROWTH AND PROFESSIONAL REFLECTION AND SELF DEVELOPMENT QUESTIONS

1) So, have you got some inkling of ways to mend all the ways you suck?

2) Do you still think your students are stupid?

3) Is it merely bad hangovers that prevent you from applying yourself to your work, or is it more of a general lack of interest?

4) Are you sure you don't want to give it up and go back to working at the Starbucks?

FINAL WORDS

Well, that's all I know. If your students won't talk at this point, it might be time to get out that waterboard.

Good luck to you, you poor bastards.

APPENDIX:

SOME ACTIVITIES FOR PROFESSIONAL DEVELOPMENT AND SELF-ABUSE

Here are some activities that will hopefully inspire the parts of your brain involved in making endless lists of questions. Proceed fearlessly yet carefully.

1) Are you ready for some serious punishment?

2) Think of 10 different questions that begin with WHAT.

3) Think of 10 different questions that begin with WHERE.

4) Think of 10 different questions that begin with WHY.

5) Think of 10 different questions in the PAST TENSE.

6) Think of 10 different questions in the PRESENT PERFECT TENSE.

7) Think of at least 30 questions on the following topics:

CARS

SPORTS

FOOD

TELEVISION

MOVIES

CRIME

HOUSES AND APARTMENTS

HOLIDAYS

WORK

HEALTH AND MEDICINE

POLITICS

UNIVERSITY

MUSIC

8) Make an entire 45 minute lesson on the topic of SPORTS, using NO PHOTOCOPIES WHATSOEVER.

9) Now make an entire lesson comprised of short speaking activities, leading up to a jolly role play involving you being a bartender and students being holiday-makers ordering drinks.

10) Make a list of questions about SPORTS suited specifically to YOUR STUDENTS ! This might involve some research on the internet to find the names of local sports teams and celebrities.

BONUS ACTIVITY: Make a realistic plan for leaving the profession of TEFL entirely, and finding a profession that offers decent salaries and benefits.

If you'd like to read more about English teaching, check out English Teacher X's memoir about his first five years of working abroad:

TO TRAVEL HOPELESSLY:

A MEMOIR ABOUT TEACHING ENGLISH ABROAD

English Teacher X, a shadowy and legendary figure in the world of Teaching English as a Foreign Language, follows up his debut book with this raw, lurid, and vivid memoir of his first five years teaching English abroad.

In 1995, after a year of aimless wandering, a young man answered an ad in a newspaper in Bangkok and inadvertently became English Teacher X, working, in the next five years, in 7 different cities in 5 different countries.

From a tropical island paradise in Thailand to an industrial hellhole of Post-Soviet Russia, English Teacher X describes, in violent imagery, the life of an English teacher overseas, encountering dishonest and exploitative employers, degenerate colleagues, corrupt police, gold-hearted prostitutes and cold-hearted "English groupies", with drugs and alcohol for all, while questing in vain for the Authentic Cultural Experience.

English Teacher X's world serves as a cautionary tale for young people going overseas to teach, or a titillating taste of the many perks of the darker side of English teaching.

BUY *TO TRAVEL HOPELESSLY*, available as a paperback and as at all major ebook retailers.

AND IF YOU WANT TO READ ENGLISH TEACHER X'S MOST BIZARRE ADVENTURES:

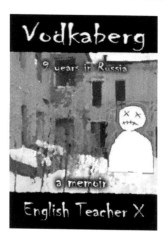

VODKABERG: NINE YEARS IN RUSSIA

In the year 2000, English Teacher X moved to the bankrupt, frozen, desolate country of Russia, seeking a quiet life.

Instead, he found himself the center of attention of the gorgeous, sexy, amoral, and abundant female population of the city of Vodkaberg, as one of the few foreign residents there.

At first bewildered and uncomfortable with the attention, he soon grew to love it and found himself settling in for a long stay of girl-chasing and vodka-drinking, and staying much, much longer than he planned.

But as the years pass, Russia begins to change and develop into a fast-growing modern oil superpower, one that is increasingly nationalistic and hostile to foreign residents.

The lives of the English teachers, however, remain mired in a perpetual adolescence of self-gratification, and as he approaches age 40, English Teacher X's conflicted emotions about his life begin to come burbling out at strange time and in bizarre ways ...

VODKABERG: NINE YEARS IN RUSSIA is a portrait of troubled people in a troubled country during a time of rapid change, and another examination of the darker side of English teaching and life abroad.

WARNING! Contains graphic and explicit depictions of all kinds of weird stuff, and bad language. And a general air of apocalyptic hopelessness.

Now available as a paperback and at all major ebook retailers.

About the Author

ENGLISH TEACHER X (www.englishteacherx.com) is a 15-year veteran of many terrible language schools all around the world.

He is also the author of ENGLISH TEACHER X GUIDE TO TEACHING ENGLISH ABROAD, as well as a memoir about his first five years of teaching in Thailand, Korea, New York, and Russia, entitled TO TRAVEL HOPELESSLY, both available as ebooks and paperbacks.

His book HOW TO SURVIVE LIVING ABROAD is a survival guide for people thinking of traveling or working in other countries.

His memoir about Russia, VODKABERG: NINE YEARS IN RUSSIA is now available.

Printed in Great Britain
by Amazon.co.uk, Ltd.,
Marston Gate.